# INDIA

### THE VEGETARIAN TABLE

# INDIA
### THE VEGETARIAN TABLE

## BY YAMUNA DEVI

### PHOTOGRAPHY BY ZEVA OELBAUM

CHRONICLE BOOKS · SAN FRANCISCO

# DEDICATION

For Jahnava Mata
Your example will last through time

Library of Congress Cataloging-in-Publication Data:
Yamuna Devi, 1942–
The vegetarian table. India/by Yamuna Devi;
photographs by Zeva Oelbaum.
p. cm.
Includes index.
ISBN 0-8118-1144-1 (hc)
1. Vegetarian cookery. 2. Cookery, Indic. I. Title.
TX837.Y36257 1997
641.5'636-DC20  96-18697
CIP

Book Design: Louise Fili Ltd.
Design Assistant: Tonya Hudson
Food Styling: Susan Ehlich

Printed in Hong Kong.

Distributed in Canada by Raincoast Books
8680 Cambie St., Vancouver, B.C. V6P 6M9

10 9 8 7 6 5 4 3 2 1

Chronicle Books
85 Second Street
San Francisco, CA 94105

Web Site: www.chronbooks.com

# CONTENTS

�֍

# ACKNOWLEDGMENTS

A MOOD OF GRATITUDE PERVADED THE WRITING OF THIS BOOK. I SPENT ALMOST A YEAR ON THE ROAD IN INDIA, EUROPE, AND AMERICA BEFORE BEGINNING A YEAR OF RECIPE DEVELOPMENT AND TESTING. While traveling, I met many knowledgeable cooks, several in India who do not speak English and will never even read this book. But to you everywhere who shared your fires, time, and hospitality, I'm grateful. Special mention must be given to Sri Padmanava Goswami of Sree Radha Raman Mandir for sharing century-old information on cuisine and kitchen standards. Sri Kanu Charan Puja Panda Samanth from the Temple of Jagannatha at Puri taught me more about ancient Orissan cuisine and techniques than I could have hoped for. In Geneva, thanks to J. P. "Animisha" Armstrong, a good friend and owner of a restaurant in Paris, for his talent and stamina, and thanks to the professionalism of Francisco Rodriguez and Gilbert Oguey of Le Richemond Traiteur and their skilled staff.

Special thanks to my agent extraordinaire, Judith Weber, for arranging this book; to Bill LeBlond at Chronicle for asking me to do this book; and to Leslie Jonath, my editor at Chronicle Books, for seeing the manuscript through to fruition.

Appreciation for the crew in Washington, D.C. runs deep: the irreplaceable Dina Sugg made life auspicious by her presence; a gentleman, Henry Schoellkopf, is both 'cool' and fun to work with; Blane Kirk, as a one-man supercrew, does too many things well to mention just one. Kim Waters-Murray, Radhika Sarin, and Lida Saeedian have great testing palates and are the best company possible. The special varieties of fine organic produce supplied by Flickerville Farm, Erhardt Organic Farm, and my friend, Erik Schwartz, from his garden, made recipe testing a real pleasure.

# VEGETARIANISM IN INDIA

✻

**I**NDIA HAS LURED TRAVELERS FOR CENTURIES. ROMANS, ARABS, EUROPEANS, AND CHINESE KNEW OF ITS OPULENCE AND CAME FOR GEMS, GOLD, MARBLE, WOOD, RICE, WHEAT, BARLEY, SUGAR, SAFFRON, PEPPER, AND SPICES. From majestic peaks in the northern Himalayas to palm-lined beaches in the south, it is a land of compelling natural beauty, diversity, and sunlight. Traveling anywhere in India is an adventure, be it by train, plane, automobile, or horse-drawn *tonga*. Today, people go there to see its ancient monuments and hear of its intriguing history. Some head to a mountain or river village for solitude and a peaceful way of life. Others want to experience riding on a caparisoned elephant and staying in a luxury palace hotel. A growing number simply go there to savor its vegetarian food.

An astounding 600 million people in India are vegetarian, over 80 percent of the population. Of the legions who put food on the table every day, most are women—wives and mothers—many with considerable skill. Among those most responsible for preserving the ancient vegetarian tradition are the male brahmana cooks who largely work in temple kitchens. Add to that the proficient professionals, who have for generations been employed by the affluent, and catering experts who cook on a large scale for entertaining, weddings, or religious holidays. Fewest in number are the chefs trained in restaurant kitchens or catering colleges; today, these are India's most innovative cooks.

I have lived and traveled in India off and on for over thirty years, and in my heart, consider it my spiritual home. Before writing this book, I returned there to recharge my batteries and explore in more depth its regional cuisines. Indian vegetarian cuisine is not one but many cuisines from many regions. This book reflects some of my travels and includes regional dishes inspired by a mixed bag of cooks—a fourth-generation wedding caterer in Lucknow, a restaurateur in Madras, a professional cook in a royal kitchen, a back-alley *dosa*-house chef in Udipi, and a gourmet family chef in Delhi. Also included are some ancient dishes gleaned from temple chefs. Rounding off the recipe selection are dishes entirely of my own devising—classics made lighter, less complex, or easier, their taste undiminished.

If you are a newcomer to Indian cooking, I strongly suggest that you work with some of the basics in the first chapter before preparing any of the recipes offered in the rest of this book. That chapter consists of a summary, with model recipes, of the ingredients and techniques of Indian cooking and the Indian table. Using it will allow you to create meals entirely to your own liking. Once you understand the process of cooking the four "staple blocks" of a meal—vegetables, dal, rice, and/or chapati flatbreads—they could easily become the mainstay of your diet, as they are in India. This chapter includes descriptions of ingredients and, especially, the typical spices and the techniques by which they are used; a recipe for chapatis, the typical everyday bread of the cuisine; recipes for the staple dals (legumes), rice, and grains; and a description of the three methods usually used for cooking vegetables with recipes for each of those ways using potatoes but, of course, applicable to almost any vegetable. Having worked through this chapter you could, without reading another page, turn out different seasonal dishes every night for months on end. On nights when time is short, you could make a whole meal of dal or soup, vegetables, and rice in a tiered steamer on one burner, practically unattended, in under an hour. This chapter is Indian cooking in a nutshell; read it, practice the techniques, and you will speak the language.

My approach to Indian food in this book is to make it easy, fresh, and beautiful. Use a pressure cooker to cut the cooking time of dal and legumes in half. If you have time to make one or two master stocks, fine, but you don't need them for most dishes in the book. Pure and fresh ingredients are hallmarks of a good Indian kitchen, not just fresh produce, but fresh masala spice blends, yogurt, flour, water, and so forth; even fresh cheese—you won't believe how easy it is to make at home, and nothing compares. Well-prepared food, Indian or otherwise, is fresh when it is served because it is fresh when it is made.

The how, what, when, why, and where of eating in India are largely influenced by the holistic science of health and well-being called Ayurveda, derived originally from the Atharvaveda, one of the four ancient sacred Vedas or bodies of knowledge delineated by the sage Vyasadeva. The oral tradition stemming from Vyasadeva was written and expanded upon in the tenth century A.D. by three principal Ayurvedic scholars, Charak, Sushruta, and Vag Bhat, and their textbooks are still being used today.

Ayurveda recognizes six tastes: sweet, sour, salty, pungent, bitter, and astringent. Not only are foods eaten or combined in a particular way for taste, but also for their effect on health. Foods considered sweet include sugary foods and milk, ghee, rice, and some fruits as well. These foods are considered harmonizing to the mind and strengthening to tissues. Sour-tasting foods, such as citrus, sour cream, yogurt, and cheese are good for the heart and digestion. Salty tastes cleanse the channels of the body and stimulate digestion. Pungent tastes, such as pepper, chilies, radishes, and ginger, improve metabolism. Bitter tastes, such as turmeric, fenugreek seeds, and bitter melon, kill bacteria and purify the blood. Astringent tastes, such as most leafy green vegetables, apples, and potatoes, help to heal wounds and dry up excess moisture and fat in the body.

The two intrinsic elements of Ayurveda dealing with combining of the six tastes and emphasis on freshness and purity are manifest on the composed Indian plate called the *thali*. Instead of being served in courses, the Indian meal is served all at once, with small portions of foods representing the six tastes artfully placed on the plate, similar in composition to vegetarian plates offered in good restaurants. For example, a *thali* may have a serving of rice in the center surrounded by one or two vegetable dishes, some kind of dal, a few spoons of yogurt raita, a little raw vegetable salad, and a slice of lemon. That simple. Add more dishes for special occasions or take some away, and some days work on a dal soup and big vegetable salad or a grain salad with pan-fried greens. Give it some practice and you'll come up with the varied, wholesome meals that satisfy your tastes and lifestyle.

The Indian vegetarian table is a gift from our ancient past. Both cooking and eating it are cause for celebration. And sharing it with others is a nice way to offer thanks to those who have kept it alive for so many generations, and an auspicious way to usher in the new millennium. *Namaste.*

CHAPTER ONE

A PRIMER ON

VEGETARIAN

COOKING

# A PRIMER ON VEGETARIAN COOKING

COOKING THROUGH THE BASICS IN THIS CHAPTER IS BOTH REWARDING AND EXCITING. AND WHEN SOME OF THEM—YOGURT, MASALA BLENDS, CHAPATIS, STOCKS, AND SAUCES—ARE APPLIED ELSEWHERE IN THE BOOK, THOSE DISHES WILL TASTE A LITTLE FRESHER, MORE LIVELY. It's my favorite chapter, because from it alone you can create sumptuous, home-style meals. Indian food need not be labor intensive. Given a tiered steamer and some practice, you can turn out a satisfying five-course meal in about an hour—all from these basic recipes.

It might be helpful to glance through the checklist below to see what items you already have on hand and what you may need to buy. Before planning a menu, you might refer to recipes for turning out perfect basmati rice, three methods for cooking vegetables, or cooking dals. If you're intimidated at the thought of making homemade cheese, the tested procedure given in this chapter will banish any fear of failure. I know more than a few very busy people who like to unwind by making a batch of chapati flatbreads; if you're a newcomer, be prepared for thirty minutes of nurturing kitchen time. With your first whiff of roasted and ground homemade spice masalas, you will see why they always taste far superior to the ready made. This is a useful chapter to refer to on many levels—occasionally or regularly.

## THE INDIAN PANTRY

Many of these pantry items are likely to be on your shelves, as they are used in many other ethnic cuisines. Most are widely available in supermarkets and natural food stores. To make authentic versions of a few dishes, you need to shop in an Indian or Middle Eastern market for split mung dal, *toor* dal and *chana* dal, *ajwain* seeds, yellow asafetida compound, fenugreek seeds, fresh curry leaves and, if you don't make them at home, curry powder, garam masala, and *sambar* masala. Don't, however, be dissuaded if you are unable to locate all of these ingredients; you can certainly cook well from this book with alternatives.

The cook with limited kitchen time might want to stock the freezer with homemade or store-bought staples such as chapatis, curry powder, garam masala, oven-dried Indian caramelized tomatoes, fried *panir* cheese, sliced mangoes and whole berries, and premeasured portions of gingered tomato sauce, vegetable stock, wet-ground paste masalas, fruit purées, and herb chutneys. For best results, store in dated, reusable freezer containers with snap-on lids.

You might consider investing in Indian-style metal storage containers for dry goods staples. Made of stainless steel, brass or copper, they come in many shapes and sizes, are long lasting and beautifully crafted. Until they are widely available, you will have to ferret them out in mail-order catalogues and in better cookware, import, and restaurant supply stores. Alternately, many types of glass jars are widely available and economical.

# A CHECKLIST OF INGREDIENTS

TO ENSURE FRESHNESS, BUY IN SMALL QUANTITIES AND STORE IN DATED, WELL-SEALED CONTAINERS. THE BRAND NAMES MENTIONED ARE ONES I USED IN TESTING THE RECIPES. SEE THE GLOSSARY FOR DESCRIPTIONS OF MANY OF THESE INGREDIENTS.

## SPICES

*ajwain* seeds

asafetida (Vani brand yellow asafetida compound)

bay leaves

cardamom pods, preferably green, or seeds

cassia leaves

cayenne powder

chilies: dried red chilies such as ancho,
   chipotle, and New Mexico; buy enough
   to crush and grind into pure chili powders

cinnamon sticks

cloves, whole

coriander seeds and ground coriander

cumin seeds and ground cumin

curry leaves

curry powder, homemade or store-bought (Bolst's brand)

dill seeds

fennel seeds

fenugreek seeds

garam masala, homemade or store-bought (Rajah brand)

mustard seeds, preferably brown

nutmeg, whole

paprika

peppercorns, black, preferably Tellicherry
   or Malabar (McCormick Seasoned Pepper)

pepper flakes, red

saffron threads

*sambar* masala, homemade or store-bought (Rajah brand)

sea salt (Herbamare Seasoned Salt)

sesame seeds

turmeric, ground

## DRIED BEANS AND PEAS FROM THE SUPERMARKET

black-eyed peas

chickpeas (garbanzo beans)

kidney beans

mung beans

split peas, yellow and green

## DALS FROM THE INDIAN MARKET

*chana* dal                    mung dal                    *toor* dal

## RICE, GRAINS, FLOURS, AND PACKAGE GOODS

all-purpose flour (King Arthur brand unbleached)

*atta*

barley

basmati rice, white and brown

couscous

cracked wheat

chapati flour

chickpea (garbanzo) flour, also called *besan*

cornmeal, stone ground

farina

plum tomatoes: canned; whole, crushed, or
     diced; preferably Italian

semolina

wheat berries

whole wheat flour

sun-dried tomatoes

tomatoes and tomato paste, canned,
     organic (Muir Glen brand)

## NUTS AND DRIED FRUIT

almonds

cashews

coconut

cranberries

currants

dates

mango

peanuts

pineapple

pistachios

raisins

## OILS AND SWEETENERS

citrus oils, pure: orange, lime, and lemon

flavored oils

fructose

ghee, homemade or store-bought
   (Purity Farms organic)

honey

maple syrup

olive oil, extra virgin

olive-oil spray

rock sugar

Sucanat (a brand of raw cane sugar)

vegetable oils, cold-pressed: corn, peanut, and sunflower

***

## MILK PRODUCTS

butter, unsalted

buttermilk

milk

yogurt

***

## FRESH PRODUCE AND AROMATICS

bell peppers, green, orange, red, and yellow

carrots

cauliflower

chilies, hot: habanero, jalapeño, serrano

eggplant

green beans

greens, such as spinach

ginger root

herbs: basil, cilantro, mint, parsley

lemons

limes, preferably Key limes

potatoes: yellow; red waxy; and baking, such as Idaho

***

## HOMEMADE STAPLES (SEE PAGE 32–40)

chapatis

chili-orange salt

concentrated vegetable stock cubes

curry powder

garam masala

ghee, plain and flavored

herb chutney cubes

oven-dried tomatoes

*panir* cheese

soured cream

yogurt cheese

# SPICES AND SEASONINGS

**S**PICES ARE THE HEARTBEAT OF THE INDIAN VEGETARIAN TRADITION. ONE OF MY INDIAN MUSIC TEACHERS LIKENED SPICES TO MUSICAL NOTES. All ragas (dishes) are brought to life with the same musical notes (spices). From asafetida to vanilla beans, more than forty spices, herbs, and seasonings are used regularly in Indian kitchens.

In classes, I am often asked why the same spices are used repeatedly in Indian dishes, whereas Western foods are made with different seasonings in each dish. According to the holistic science of Ayurveda, aside from flavor, not only *what* spices are used, but *how* they are used is important. For example, asafetida and ginger help break down the enzymes in protein-rich foods such as dal and *panir* cheese. When cumin, fennel, and coriander seeds are toasted, they help boost the fire of digestion. Turmeric is a blood purifier. By adjusting the amount and relationship of spices, you get not rubber-stamp flavor, but results elusive enough to stump a trained palate.

All spice seeds do not act the same over heat, and it's important to add them to a spice blend at the right time. Mustard seeds are fried until they pop, turn gray, and jump out of the pan; keep them in place with a spatter screen. Whole cumin, fennel, *ajwain*, and coriander seeds are toasted until they darken a few shades and become fragrant. Fresh ginger and hot chilies are best fried in ghee or oil, not only because of their moisture content, but also because the flavor of a little of these infused oils goes a long way. Because ground spices burn easily over heat, it's best as a rule to turn them into moist purées before adding them to oil. Simply cook them until the liquid has evaporated and then fry them in oil.

A few other ways to use Indian spices:
- Dry-roast cumin seeds until fragrant and crush coarsely; sprinkle on salads and steamed, baked, or pan-fried vegetables
- Crush whole spice seeds and fry them in a little oil; off the heat, whisk in fresh lemon or lime juice for refreshing vinaigrettes
- To make protein-rich foods more digestible, fry fresh ginger and asafetida in a little ghee or oil and add it to the dish
- To make a quick spice-infused oil, warm a few tablespoons of spices in ½ cup of oil for 20 minutes; drain

## CHONKS

The most widely used technique is called a *chonk* or *bhoona*, and you'll find it used in many recipes in this book. To make a *chonk*, spices and seasonings are fried either dry or in oil, until their aroma and flavor intensifies. Spice seeds are used whole, crushed, or ground into wet pastes. When subjected to heat, the volatile oils dormant in the spices come to life. Depending on the desired result, a *chonk* is made in varying intensities of heat, from moderately high to very low. For example, a Bengali spice-seed *chonk* might be flash-fried over lively heat; a Marawari wet-paste *chonk* might be fried over very low heat for ten minutes and stirred constantly to prevent scorching. A *chonk* may be added at the beginning, middle, or end of cooking.

Spice-flavored ghee can also be made with a *chonk*. Just as herbs and concentrated vegetable or fruit juices are used to make flavored oils, spices make outstanding flavored ghee. Easy to master on the first try, you simply make a *chonk* in a dry pan, add unsalted butter, and melt it. As it simmers, the water and casein (milk solids) separate from the pure butterfat. You will be impressed with the excellent flavor of a *chonk*-infused ghee.

✵

## MASALA BLENDS

The Hindi word *masala* is used in other cuisines, but in India it simply means spices. Masalas are used in a myriad ways, not only for the flavor, color, taste, and consistency they give a dish, but also for their medicinal value. Masala blends fall into two broad categories: dry powders and wet pastes. Today, three powdered blends are widely used in many regional cuisines—curry powder, garam masala, and *sambar* masala.

It's a toss-up which is better, homemade South Indian curry powder or North Indian garam masala, for both are hallmarks of fine Indian cuisine. Many spices can be used in a curry powder, up to twenty in complex blends. Some cooks roast each spice separately for a requisite amount of time before grinding them.

Second only to curry powder in popularity, fragrant garam masala is used in many regional cuisines, but particularly in central and northern ones. Garam translates as "warm" or "hot," and masala as a "spice mixture." Ginger, cardamom, black pepper, cinnamon, cloves, and chilies, prominent ingredients in garam masalas, are considered warm in nature and fuel the fire of digestion. So, aside from the flavor and aroma they impart to a dish, they are especially beneficial when used in protein-rich legume and *panir* dishes.

# CURRY POWDER

MAKES ABOUT ¾ CUP

**T**HERE ARE TWO IMPORTANT FLAVORS IN THIS TIME-SAVING, SEVEN-INGREDIENT CURRY POWDER: FENUGREEK SEEDS AND FRESH CURRY LEAVES, AVAILABLE AT INDIAN GROCERS. FRESH CURRY LEAVES ARE SUPPLE AND INTENSELY FRAGRANT; DON'T BOTHER WITH DRIED LEAVES, THEY ARE DULL AND LIFELESS. DEPENDING ON HOW MUCH YOU USE, YOU MAY WANT TO DOUBLE OR TRIPLE THIS RECIPE — I INVARIABLY END UP GIVING AWAY AS MUCH AS I MAKE.

½ cup coriander seeds

20 to 25 fresh curry leaves

2 tablespoons cumin seeds

1½ tablespoons brown mustard seeds

1 teaspoon fenugreek seeds

2½ tablespoons turmeric

1 to 3 dried chipotle chilies or
    ½ tablespoon pure chili powder
    (optional)

Warm a heavy skillet over medium-low heat. Add the coriander, curry leaves, cumin, mustard, and fenugreek, and if you are using them, the whole chipotles, and toast, stirring occasionally, until the curry leaves are crackling dry and the spices are fragrant; 15 to 25 minutes. When cool, break the chilies into pieces, and transfer the mixture to a blender or spice mill. Reduce to a powder, then shake through a fine sieve; discard the roughage. Mix in the turmeric and the optional chili powder. Use while fresh or store in an airtight container in a cool place for a few weeks.

# GARAM MASALA

�֍

MAKES ABOUT ⅔ CUP

IF YOU ONLY MAKE ONE SPICE BLEND AT HOME, MAKE IT GARAM MASALA. YOU CAN TOAST THE SPICES ON THE BACK BURNER WHILE YOU CUT VEGETABLES. WHEN YOU GRIND THE SPICES, THE MOST DELICIOUS AROMAS WILL FILL YOUR KITCHEN. TWO VARIATIONS ARE OFFERED HERE—THE FIRST A LITTLE PEPPERY AND THE SECOND SLIGHTLY SWEET. WE USED THE LATTER IN TESTING MOST RECIPES.

Preheat a heavy skillet over medium-low heat. Add all of the ingredients and dry-toast the spices, stirring occasionally, until they darken slightly, about 15 minutes. Transfer to a coffee grinder or blender, and grind to a powder. Sift through a fine sieve, discarding the roughage. Use while fresh or store in an airtight container for up to a month.

VARIATION: To either of the above, you might add: 1 or 2 bay leaves, ½ teaspoon *ajwain* seeds, and after grinding the other spices, ¼ teaspoon freshly ground nutmeg.

*Punjabi-Style Garam Masala*

¼ cup cumin seeds

⅓ cup coriander seeds

½ tablespoon cardamom seeds

½ tablespoon black peppercorns

15 whole cloves

2-inch piece cinnamon stick

*Gujarati-Style Garam Masala*

½ cup coriander seeds

3 tablespoons fennel seeds

1 tablespoon brown mustard seeds

1 teaspoon cardamom seeds

10 whole cloves

½ teaspoon red pepper flakes

2-inch piece cinnamon stick

# SAMBAR MASALA

MAKES ABOUT ¼ CUP

GENEROUS AMOUNT OF THIS MASALA IS USED IN THE SOUTH INDIAN DAL SOUP CALLED **SAMBAR** (SEE PAGE 86), BUT A LITTLE SPRINKLED INTO ALMOST ANY POT OF BEANS OR DAL GIVES IT A KICK. THIS **SAMBAR** MASALA IS FRESH, MILD, AND VERY EASY TO LIKE, BUT AS IT YIELDS A MERE QUARTER CUP, YOU CAN INCREASE OR DECREASE THE QUANTITIES OF ANY INGREDIENT TO SUIT YOUR TASTE WHEN YOU MAKE THE NEXT BATCH.

Preheat a heavy skillet over medium-low heat; add everything but the turmeric and chili powder. Toast the ingredients until they are fragrant and lightly toasted, about 15 minutes. Transfer to a blender or spice mill and reduce to a fine powder. Sprinkle through a fine sieve; discard the roughage. Mix in the turmeric and chili powder. Store in an airtight jar and use as needed.

*2 tablespoons coriander seeds*

*1 tablespoon chana dal*

*1 tablespoon toor dal*

*1 teaspoon cumin seeds*

*1 teaspoon black peppercorns*

*2 teaspoons brown mustard seeds*

*½ teaspoon fenugreek seeds*

*2-inch piece cinnamon stick*

*15 dry or fresh curry leaves*

*1 teaspoon turmeric*

*½ tablespoon pure chili powder*

# ORANGE-CHILI SALT

MAKES ABOUT ⅓ CUP

THIS SWEET-HOT SALT IS A FINE ACCOMPANIMENT TO MANY PLAIN FOODS, FROM STIR-FRIED GREENS TO STEAMED RICE. GOOD INDIAN CHILIES SUCH AS **RESHHAMPATTI**, KASHMIRI, NELLORE, OR GOAN ARE NOT AVAILABLE HERE, SO I RELY ON SOME OF THE FINE VARIETIES THAT ARE, AMONG THEM, NEW MEXICO, ANCHO, ARBOL AND, MY FAVORITE, SMOKE-FLAVORED CHIPOTLE. GROUND IN A SALT MILL, THE SALT IS FLECKED WITH COLOR FROM THE ORANGE ZEST AND CHILIES; GROUND IN A BLENDER, IT FLOWS BRICK RED.

*2 dried chipotle chilies*

*¼ cup coarse sea salt crystals*

*2 tablespoons dried orange zest*

*1 tablespoon crushed rock sugar or*
*    coarse sugar crystals*

*¼ teaspoon cardamom seeds*

Pan-toast the dried chilies briefly until they are slightly fragrant and brittle, about 1 minute. When cool, process in a blender or spice mill until crushed into flakes. Combine them in a bowl with the salt, zest, sugar, and cardamom, and mix. Transfer to a salt mill and grind as you would plain rock salt. Alternately, place the pan-toasted chilies in a blender and process until crushed. Add the remaining ingredients and process for several minutes. Pour through a fine-meshed strainer; discard the leftover flakes. Transfer to a salt shaker for the table or store in an airtight jar.

# PASTE MASALAS

NOTHER WAY SPICES AND AROMATICS ARE USED IS IN WET-GROUND PURÉES, SIMPLY CALLED PASTE MASALAS. THIN PURÉES OF FRESH GINGER, HOT CHILIES, HERBS, OR SPICE SEEDS ARE USED EITHER SINGLY OR BLENDED. IF YOU WANT TO EXPLORE COOKING WITH PASTE MASALAS BUT ARE ON A TIGHT SCHEDULE, MAKE UP A FEW AND KEEP THEM ON HAND IN THE REFRIGERATOR OR FREEZER. A SPOON OR TWO OF ANY PASTE MASALA NEED ONLY BE FRIED UNTIL FRAGRANT, WITH ADDED WATER OR LIQUID, WITH OR WITHOUT OIL, AND THEN USED TO SEASON A DISH. LIKE THE POWDERED SPICE BLENDS, CURRY POWDER AND GARAM MASALA, A COMPLEX WET-PASTE MASALA BLEND GIVES A DISH DEEP, LAYERED FLAVORS. WET MASALAS HOLD IN A REFRIGERATOR FOR A FEW DAYS, AND FROZEN IN TWO-TABLESPOON ICE-CUBE TRAY PORTIONS, FOR UP TO A MONTH.

## CHILI-SPICE MASALA

MAKES ⅔ CUP

Combine all the ingredients in a blender jar and blend until smooth. Use immediately or refrigerate or freeze as desired.

After trying this one, you'll probably come up with blends of your own, perhaps inspired by some especially tender ginger root or fragrant herbs.

*2 or 3 green chilies*

*a 2-inch piece ginger, sliced*

*2 teaspoons cumin seeds*

*2 tablespoons coriander seeds*

*1 teaspoon fennel seeds*

*½ teaspoon turmeric*

*½ cup water*

*2 tablespoons vegetable or nut oil*

*½ teaspoon salt*

*several fresh curry leaves or a few spoons
    of chopped cilantro (optional)*

# RICE, GRAINS, AND BREAD

## BASMATI RICE

**M**ANY STRAINS OF RICE ARE WIDELY EATEN IN INDIA, INCLUDING FINE-GRAINED **JEERA**, THICKER, GOLDEN-HUED **SELA**, MANGO-SCENTED **AMBE MOHUR**, AND **PUNNI** RICE FROM TAMIL NADU, BUT NONE IS QUITE AS REVERED WORLDWIDE AS BASMATI. SOMETIMES CALLED THE KING OF RICES, BASMATI IS POPULAR IN ALL REGIONS. THE GRAINS ARE LONG AND SLIGHTLY CURVED, TAPERING TO POINTED ENDS. WHEN COOKED, THE GRAINS EXPAND FOUR TIMES THEIR LENGTH AND GIVE OFF A BUTTERY FRAGRANCE. PLAIN BASMATI MAY BE BOILED OR STEAMED.

## BOILED BASMATI RICE

SERVES 2

1 cup basmati rice

8 cups water

pinch salt

a few drops of ghee or oil

Rinse the rice in several changes of water until it runs clear. Soak the rice in water for 15 to 20 minutes to allow the grains to expand by 25 percent and to relax. Bring the water, salt, and ghee or oil to a boil in a large, nonstick saucepan. Stir in the rinsed, soaked, and drained rice and cook until almost tender; 7 to 10 minutes. Drain well and return the rice to the hot cooking pot to finish cooking and dry out slowly; at least 5 minutes.

## STEAMED BASMATI RICE

SERVES 2

1 cup basmati rice

1⅔ cups water

¼ teaspoon salt

a few drops of ghee or oil

Rinse the rice in several changes of water until it runs clear. Soak the rice in water for 15 to 20 minutes to allow the grains to expand by 25 percent and relax. Bring the water, salt, and ghee or oil to a boil in a nonstick saucepan. Stir in the rice, cover, and reduce the heat to the lowest setting. Cook until almost tender, 10 to 12 minutes. (Add sprinkles of water if the water is completely absorbed.) Turn off the heat and set aside for 5 minutes to continue cooking the rice in its own steam until each grain is fully cooked. Fluff the grains with a fork to allow them to separate and dry out.

## RICE WITH GREENS

Stem, devein, and finely slice 12 ounces of collard greens, Swiss chard, or kale. Dry roast 1 teaspoon of cumin seeds in a large, nonstick skillet over moderately high heat. Add the greens and 2 tablespoons of golden raisins and stir-fry until bright green and wilted, 3 or 4 minutes. Stir in 2 tablespoons of toasted slivered almonds and season with salt and pepper. Add this mixture to the cooked rice.

*1 recipe Boiled or Steamed Basmati Rice (page 24)*

## YELLOW RICE WITH BABY PEAS

Add a pinch of turmeric to the cooking water; it will lend color, not flavor. Fold ½ cup baby peas into the almost-cooked rice, set aside to warm for 5 minutes, and fluff. Garnish with chopped mint.

*1 recipe Boiled or Steamed Basmati Rice (page 24)*

## RICE WITH FRIED SPICES

Heat 1 tablespoon of ghee or oil in a pan over moderate heat. Add 1 teaspoon each of cumin, fennel, and coriander seeds and fry until toasted. Add the spices to the cooked rice and garnish with chopped cilantro.

*1 recipe Boiled or Steamed Basmati Rice (page 24)*

## FRAGRANT RICE

Add a 1-inch piece of cinnamon stick, a few cloves and whole peppercorns, 2 or 3 green cardamom pods, and ¼ of a bay leaf to the water when steaming or boiling; serve with or without the spices.

*1 recipe Boiled or Steamed Basmati Rice (page 24)*

# WHEAT BERRY PILAF

❉

SERVES 4 TO 6

CALLED **GEHUN PILAU**, THIS TOOTHSOME WHOLE-GRAIN PILAF IS A GOOD ALTERNATIVE TO BASMATI RICE IN ANY INDIAN-STYLE MEAL, AND EQUALLY NICE ON A COMPOSED VEGETARIAN DINNER PLATE. FOR CLASSIC INDIAN SERVICE, PLACE A MOUND OF PILAF IN THE CENTER OF A 12- TO 14-INCH DINNER PLATE OR LARGE METAL **THALI**, AND SURROUND IT WITH SMALL PORTIONS OF SEVERAL SIDE DISHES SUCH AS VEGETABLES, BEAN DISHES, SOUPS OR SALADS. FOR AN EVERYDAY VEGETABLE PLATE, SURROUND A MOUND OF PILAF WITH AN ASSORTMENT OF GRILLED, STEAMED, OR BAKED VEGETABLES.

1½ cups wheat berries

1 tablespoon finely chopped fresh ginger

1 or 2 hot green chilies, finely chopped

2 carrots, chopped

2 stalks celery, chopped

2 cassia or bay leaves

zest and juice of 1 lime or lemon

1½ tablespoons flavored or plain
    olive oil

½ tablespoon brown mustard seeds

¼ teaspoon asafetida (optional)

3 tablespoons chopped cilantro or
    flat-leaf parsley

2 tablespoons chopped fresh mint

salt and freshly ground pepper

Soak the wheat berries either overnight in a pot of water or by the quick-soak method: cover the wheat berries with 2 inches of water in a pot, boil for 2 minutes, remove from the heat, cover, and set aside for 1 hour.

Drain off the soaking water and cover with fresh water by ½ an inch. Add the ginger, chilies, carrots, celery, cassia or bay leaves, and citrus zest. Cover and simmer until the grains are tender and slightly puffed, about 1 hour. Drain off excess liquid.

Heat the olive oil in a small pan over moderate heat. Add the mustard seeds and cook, partially covered, until they sputter and pop. Sprinkle in the asafetida and, within seconds, pour the mustard-infused oil into the wheat berries. Stir in the lemon juice and herbs, and season with salt and pepper to taste.

# CHAPATIS

MAKES 1 DOZEN LARGE CHAPATIS

EATEN FOR THOUSANDS OF YEARS, CHAPATIS STILL REMAIN INDIA'S MOST POPULAR FLATBREAD, THE WHOLE WHEAT EQUIVALENT OF MEXICAN FLOUR TORTILLAS. MADE WITH ONLY FLOUR AND WATER, THEY ARE ROLLED OUT PAPER-THIN TO ¼-INCH THICK, IN 5- TO 12-INCH CIRCLES. INITIALLY BAKED ON A GRIDDLE UNTIL ALMOST COOKED, THEY ARE THEN PUFFED INTO STEAM-FILLED BALLOONS OVER DIRECT HEAT, BECOMING FLAME-TOASTED ON THE OUTSIDE. ❋ INDIAN COOKS PREFER USING **ATTA**, A GRANULAR FLOUR MILLED FROM SOFT INDIAN WHEAT THAT YIELDS DELICATE, REFINED FLATBREADS; IT'S AVAILABLE AT INDIAN GROCERS. TWO COMMERCIAL ALTERNATIVES FOR CHAPATIS ARE GARDEN OF EATIN'S ORGANIC WHOLE WHEAT TORTILLAS AND ALVARADO STREET BAKERY'S SPROUTED WHEAT TOR-TILLAS, BOTH SOLD IN NATURAL FOOD STORES.

*4 cups (about 1 pound) chapati or durum wheat flour*
*½ teaspoon salt (optional)*
*about 1½ cups warm water*
*unbleached flour for rolling out*
*optional ghee or butter*

Mix the flour and optional salt in a food processor or large bowl. With the machine running or while mixing by hand, dribble in water to make a shaggy ball of dough. Adding flour or water as necessary, make a medium-firm dough that is smooth and elastic; knead for 1 minute in the processor or several minutes by hand. Set aside, covered, for 30 minutes to 1 hour.

Preheat a large single- or double-burner griddle over moderate heat for several minutes.

Divide the dough into 12 flat patties and set aside, covered. Using only enough unbleached flour to facilitate shaping, roll a pattie into an evenly thin, 8-inch round. Brush the excess flour from both sides and slip it on the hot griddle. Cook until the top surface lightens and small brown spots fleck the underside; flip over and cook on the second side; 2 or 3 minutes in all. (Pressing the surface of a partially cooked chapati with a folded towel helps it to puff up.) Remove the griddle from the heat. Holding the chapati with tongs, place it over a gas burner set on high heat. (If using electricity, place under a broiler.) Within 30 seconds, it will fill with steam, puff into a balloon, and finish cooking; flip over. When both sides are flecked with char spots, transfer to a towel-lined container to deflate; if desired, brush with ghee or butter. Serve hot or keep in a towel-covered container while cooking the remaining chapatis.

To store: cool, wrap, and refrigerate for up to 3 days; freeze for up to 1 month.

# DALS

✵

**A**NY TYPE OF DRIED BEAN, LENTIL, OR SPLIT PEA IS CALLED **DAL**, AND IT'S CENTRAL TO THE INDIAN VEGETARIAN DIET. Along with rice, it is eaten daily in puréed soups and whole bean dishes, but also in an amazing variety of breads, crêpes, salads, dumplings, and even sweets. Dal contains important amino acids that are lacking in rice. It is high in protein, fiber, and complex carbohydrates, low in fat, and cholesterol free.

Surprisingly, only four varieties of dal are widely used in India. Most popular in the east are *chana* dal and *kala chana* dal, split and whole Bengal *gram*, a smaller cousin of the chickpea. In northern and western India, both split and whole mung beans, called *chilke* mung dal and *sabat* mung dal, are favored. *Urad* dal or black *gram* is similar in shape and size to black beans, and is much loved from Punjab in the north to Uttar Pradesh in the east. Split pigeon peas, called *arhar* or *toor* dal, are eaten in the west and the south. To a lesser degree, black-eyed peas and lentils are also used in many regions. Unlike many beans popular in Western cuisines, all of these dals do not require soaking time, cook quickly, and are easy to digest; they're available at Indian and Middle Eastern markets. Many varieties of old-world beans are now widely available and they taste good seasoned like dal. A few that I use often include Christmas limas, Steuben Yellow Eyes, Jacob's cattle, and Calypso; these and other western beans should be soaked overnight in water to cover by 3 inches and then drained.

One type of dal dish is dry textured, cooked so that the dal grains remain whole and separate, like rice. This kind of dal can be served hot or at room temperature, like a bean salad. Add any spice-sautéed or roasted seasonal vegetable to the dal to make it the center of a meal. This works well with small *chana* or split, husked mung dal, but also with larger, flavorful old-world legumes such as Appaloosa, China Yellow, Rattlesnake, Calypso, Tongues of Fire, Snowcap, Steuben Yellow Eyes, or Christmas lima beans. These varieties are available under a few labels now: Dean & DeLuca, Melissa's, Esculent Heirloom, and in bulk, and often organic, at large natural food stores.

From there, make dals into gravies, stews, textured or blended cream soups, smooth light soups, or simply use the broth of dal. Given the number of dals available and the options possible, you can really go to town with variety.

✵

## BASIC DAL

No matter what variety or consistency of dal dish you intend to make, you have to cook the dried beans to tenderness first. Always sort through them and remove any stones or foreign matter, then rinse under running water until it runs clear. The older the dal, the longer it takes to cook. Add salt when the dal is cooked.

To cook an unsoaked dal or any soaked, drained beans, cover them with 3 inches of water in a saucepan. Add a piece of ginger, pinch of turmeric, and a little ghee or oil. Bring to a boil, then reduce heat and boil gently, partially covered, until the dal is tender and the consistency you want. You can make dal a day or so ahead of serving time. Just before serving, for both flavor and to assist in digestion, add chopped herbs and season it with a *chonk*, as described on page 30.

# VEGETABLE STOCK WITH BEANS

MAKES ABOUT 8 CUPS

I N INDIA, VEGETABLE TRIMMINGS ARE MORE LIKELY TO END UP AS BRUNCH FOR A STREET COW THAN AS INGREDIENTS IN A STOCKPOT. BUT REJECTED SEEDS, OUTER LEAVES, OR STALKS MAY BE TRANS-FORMED INTO A STOCK AND USED FOR THE SPECIFIC PURPOSE OF REINFORCING FLAVOR. FOR EXAMPLE, I USE A PUMPKIN SEED–PUMPKIN SKIN STOCK IN PUMPKIN **KITCHEREE** AND CORN STALK–CORN HUSK STOCK IN CORN CHOWDER. ❋ THIS IS AN EXAMPLE OF A NUTRITIOUS AND FLAVORFUL VEGETABLE AND LEGUME STOCK. IT IS INSPIRED BY THE EVER-PRACTICAL AND INGENIOUS INDIAN COOKS WHO TURN OUT TWO DISHES ON ONE BURNER IN RECORD TIME. THEY SIMMER CHUNKS OF VEGETABLES AND WHOLE BEANS IN ONE POT, SERVING THE BROTH AS A LIGHT SOUP AND THE COOKED SOLIDS AS AN EARTHY MAIN DISH OF BEANS AND VEGETABLES. THIS STOCK GETS ITS FLAVOR FROM CHICKPEAS AND WINTER VEGETABLES, BUT YOU COULD USE WHOLE MUNG BEANS OR ANY VARIETY OF LEGUMES AND ANY COMBINATION OF SEASONAL VEGETABLES. SERVE THE STOCK ON ITS OWN AS A CONSOMMÉ, OR TRANSFORM IT INTO A BISQUE BY ADDING SOME PURÉED VEGETABLES AND LEGUMES BACK INTO IT. SEASON THE COOKED VEGETABLES AND CHICKPEAS WITH SALT, PEPPER, FRESH HERBS AND A **CHONK**, AS DESCRIBED ON PAGE 30.

Place the washed vegetable trimmings in a food processor and chop finely. Tie the vegetables, peppercorns, fennel seeds, ginger, and curry or bay leaves in a square of cheesecloth. Drain the chickpeas, and place them in a large stockpot along with vegetable trimmings in cheesecloth and water; bring to a boil over high heat. Reduce the heat and, skimming the surface as necessary, simmer uncovered for about 30 to 45 minutes. Add the squash, carrots, and celery, and cook slowly until the beans are tender, from 45 minutes to 1 hour. Season with salt. Strain the stock, pressing the bag of cheesecloth with the back of a spoon to extract as much liquid as possible. Add the cilantro to the stock.

Use as suggested above, or cool and refrigerate. Freeze in ice-cube trays or premeasured ½- or 1-cup portions.

1 quart vegetable trimmings, such as
    green beans, celery root, yams,
    squash, parsnips, or potatoes
½ tablespoon peppercorns
½ tablespoon fennel seeds
1-inch piece fresh ginger root, sliced
3 sprigs fresh curry leaves or 2 bay leaves
1½ cups chickpeas, soaked overnight in
    3 times their volume of water
4 quarts water
1 Butternut or Delicata squash, peeled,
    seeded, and cubed
3 carrots, scraped and thickly sliced
3 celery stalks with top leaves, sliced
salt to taste
⅓ cup chopped cilantro

# INDIAN-STYLE VEGETABLES

2 TO 4 SERVINGS

**I**NDIAN VEGETABLE COOKERY IS A TRADITION AS DIVERSE AS THE PEOPLE WHO USE IT. RECIPES AND TECHNIQUES ARE HANDED DOWN FOR GENERATIONS AND DIFFERENTLY NAMED IN DIFFERENT REGIONS. But you needn't stick to Indian classics for a sumptuous table. Go on your own journey of discovery using three simple methods for cooking vegetables. All three methods use the same ingredients, but simply by changing the heat source and intensity, adding moisture, changing pan size or the cut of the vegetables you can end up with dry, moist, puréed, stewed, gravied, or brothy vegetable dishes. The more you experiment with these methods, the more inspired you'll become.

### METHOD ONE: DRY-TEXTURED VEGETABLES

In this method, the vegetables are cooked with very little added water. Small pieces of uniformly cut vegetables—julienned thick or thin, diced, finely shredded, or in thin diagonal slices—are sautéed in seasoned ghee or oil in a heavy-bottomed pan until they are partially cooked and browned. As they cook, turn them frequently or shake the pan so that the vegetables brown evenly and do not stick. From here on, you have two options. The first is to reduce the heat and fry until the vegetables are tender and golden. The second is to add sprinkles of liquid, and by adjusting the heat, as necessary, in the moderate range, cook to tenderness in an almost dry pan, the moisture evaporated off. This method works well with root vegetables and starchy vegetables, such as potatoes, yams, colocassia, plantains, sweet potatoes, parsnips, carrots, celeriac, and eggplant, and some leafy greens, such as kale, chard, cabbage, and Asian greens.

### METHOD TWO: VEGETABLES COOKED IN A SEASONED STOCK

With this method, the vegetables may be served dry, in a stew, or aromatic stock. Use medium-sized pieces of uniformly cut vegetables—cubed, turned, sliced, or roll-cut. Briefly sauté the vegetables in seasoned ghee or oil, then add 2 to 4 cups of water. For example, depending on the featured vegetable or vegetable combination, use 1½ to 2½ cups water for the stew or 4 or more cups for the broth. Cook gently until the vegetables are tender. This method is suitable for many vegetables, including cauliflower, summer and winter squash, beets, bell peppers, new potatoes, chayote, and corn.

### METHOD THREE: PRECOOKED VEGETABLES, SEASONED WITH A **CHONK**

This method works well for almost any vegetable and for almost any finished texture. Steam, grill, bake, boil, fry, or roast a vegetable until almost tender; cut into a desired shape. Make a spice-seed or wet-paste *chonk* over brisk heat. Add the vegetables, and sauté briefly. Serve as is, or add any quantity of water, stock, yogurt, soured cream, nut milk, or creamed coconut to yield a broth, sauce, gravy, or glaze.

To familiarize yourself with these three cooking methods, use the ingredients below to make the sample recipes that follow.

# INDIAN-STYLE HASH BROWNS

### METHOD ONE

Cut the potatoes into ¼-inch dice. Heat the ghee or oil in a heavy, nonstick skillet over moderately high heat. When it's hot, in rapid succession, add the mustard seeds, cumin seeds, some minced green chili or pepper flakes, and grated ginger. When the mustard seeds pop, sprinkle in the asafetida, and a few seconds later, add the potatoes. Cook, shaking the pan, until the potatoes are two-thirds cooked and browned, about 10 minutes. Reduce the heat to low, add the turmeric and a sprinkle of water. Cover and steam-fry until tender and lightly browned. Season with salt and pepper and garnish with cilantro.

# POTATOES IN MUSTARD STOCK

### METHOD TWO

Cut Yukon Gold or red potatoes into 1-inch cubes. Purée the mustard seeds, green chili, ginger, and turmeric with 1 cup of water. Heat half of the ghee or oil in a heavy, nonstick saucepan over moderately high heat. When hot, add the cumin seeds and fry until they darken a bit. Add the asafetida and, within seconds, the mustard mixture. Cook until the liquid evaporates. Add the remaining ghee or oil. Add the potatoes and sauté for 5 minutes, stirring often. Pour in 2½ cups of water and bring to a boil. Reduce the heat and gently cook until the potatoes are tender. Season with salt and pepper and stir in the cilantro.

# CREAMY YOGURT POTATOES

### METHOD THREE

Bake or boil the potatoes until tender. Peel and cut the potatoes into ½-inch cubes. Heat the ghee or oil in a heavy, nonstick skillet over moderate heat. When warm, add the cumin seeds and pepper flakes and fry until they darken slightly. Add the asafetida and turmeric and fry for a few seconds, then add the potatoes. Pan-fry the mixture until hot and remove from the heat. Season with salt and pepper, fold in ⅔ cup stirred yogurt or sour cream, and garnish with cilantro.

*1 pound potatoes or other vegetable*

*1 or 2 tablespoons ghee or*
*    unrefined corn oil*

*1 to 2 teaspoons brown mustard seeds*
*    (for methods one and two)*

*1 teaspoon cumin seeds*

*hot green chilies or dried red pepper*
*    flakes, as desired*

*½ tablespoon grated fresh ginger root, or*
*    as desired (for methods one and two)*

*¼ teaspoon yellow asafetida, or*
*    as desired*

*½ teaspoon turmeric*

*water, as suggested*

*salt and freshly ground pepper*

*2 tablespoons chopped cilantro*

# HOMEMADE STAPLES

✳

## GHEE

**G**HEE—CLARIFIED BUTTER—IS AN AMAZING SUBSTANCE. MELTED, IT POURS LIKE LIQUID GOLD. AT ROOM TEMPERATURE, IT IS SEMISOFT AND CREAMY. More intense than that of fine butter, its aroma is sweet, almost caramel-like. Unlike butter, it can be kept at room temperature for months and heated to frying temperatures without burning. Ghee takes only moments of hands-on time to make at home and, because of its exceptional taste, a little goes a long way. Ghee is a Good Thing.

Modern research offers some facts about ghee, which is to the Indian diet what olive oil is to the Mediterranean diet. It's a source of beta-carotene and vitamins A, D, E, and K. Beta-carotene and vitamin E are both valuable antioxidants, helpful in preventing injury to the body. Ghee contains between 4 and 5 percent linoleic acid, an essential fatty acid often lacking in a vegetarian diet. Because the casein in butter has been removed, ghee is lactose free and contains no oxidized cholesterol. According to the *Charak Samhita*, an ancient Ayurvedic text on health, "ghee is good for the eyes, stimulates digestion, supports skin glow, enhances memory and stamina, and helps to promote longevity."

Both ghee and clarified butter are made the same way, the only difference being that the former is completely clarified, pure butterfat and the latter is not. To make ghee, unsalted butter is slowly heated until its roughly 8 percent water content has evaporated off, and its 4 percent protein casein solids separate from the pure butterfat. (Because all of the water and casein are not entirely removed, clarified butter must be refrigerated to prevent spoilage.)

Ayurveda has long recognized that, when spices are fried in ghee, as in the technique called a *chonk*, their activity and utility is potentiated many times over. In granny kitchen terms, it's said "good ghee, good *chonk*." Unlike butter, which burns at high temperatures, ghee can be used to sauté, pan-fry, or deep-fry up to 375°F. It can be used in place of butter for pastry dough or dribbled over plain foods when you want a lot of flavor with very little fat.

Shoppers will have to look around to find good quality ghee on store shelves. Like oil, it does not require refrigeration, but must be stored properly—ideally in a cool, dark place in a well-sealed container. The only brand of ready-made ghee I recommend is organic, from Purity Farms Inc., and is sold in many large natural food stores.

The quality of the ghee rests on the quality of butter, so use the best available. It's so easy to prepare that I rarely purchase it. Like other fine quality oils in my kitchen, I keep a small amount of plain and a few varieties of flavored ghee on my kitchen shelves.

## HOMEMADE GHEE

Place the butter in a heavy-bottomed saucepan and bring it to a gentle boil over moderate heat. Initially, it will froth and foam, and then begin to settle down. At this point, reduce the heat to low. Stirring occasionally, cook until a thin crust begins to form on the surface and milky white solids fall to the bottom of the pan. Eventually, they will turn from white to fawn colored. When the ghee is clear, translucent and pleasantly fragrant, it is done. Toward the end of the process, ghee burns quickly, so watch it carefully. Burnt ghee takes on a granular texture when chilled and turns a dull beige color, because the lactose sugars have gone from caramelized to burned.

Pour the hot ghee through a sieve lined with 2 thicknesses of unbleached, plain paper towels. Avoid letting any moisture or water into the ghee, as this promotes bacterial growth.

To make flavored ghee, add 1 or 2 of the following ingredients to the pot with each pound of unsalted butter: 6 sprigs of fresh curry leaves; 20 whole cloves; a 3-inch cinnamon stick; 1½ tablespoons whole peppercorns; a 2-inch piece ginger root, sliced; 1 or 2 whole dried chilies, such as chipotle, New Mexico, or ancho; a few long strips of lemon or lime zest; a small bunch of cilantro or mint; or 2 tablespoons whole cumin, fennel, or coriander seeds.

*1 pound unsalted butter makes about 1¾ cups ghee and cooks in about 30 minutes*

*2 pounds unsalted butter makes about 3½ cups ghee and cooks in about 1 hour*

*5 pounds unsalted butter makes about 9 cups ghee and cooks in 2 to 3 hours*

# YOGURT AND YOGURT CHEESE

✺

CALLED **DAHI** AND **DEHIN**, YOGURT AND YOGURT CHEESE HAVE BEEN STAPLES IN INDIAN HOUSE-
HOLDS FOR THOUSANDS OF YEARS. ON THE TABLE, YOGURT IS WIDELY POPULAR IN LITTLE RAITA
SALADS AND **LASSI** YOGURT SHAKES. IN THE KITCHEN, IT IS VALUED AS A SOURING AGENT AND FOR THE
BODY AND CREAMY TEXTURE IT LENDS TO DISHES, MUCH LIKE SOUR CREAM IS IN THE WEST. **DEHIN** IS
NOT REALLY A CHEESE, JUST YOGURT DRAINED OF WHEY UNTIL IT IS THICK AND RICH. ✺ TO MAKE
HOMEMADE YOGURT, YOU NEED MILK AND A LIVE YOGURT CULTURE, ONE DEVOID OF ADDITIVES, STABI-
LIZERS, OR GELATIN. IF YOU ARE COOKING WITH YOGURT, A HIGHER FAT CONTENT IS PREFERRED
BECAUSE IT IS LESS LIKELY TO BREAK OR BECOME GRANULAR OVER HEAT. TO SEE HOW DELICIOUS
YOGURT CAN BE IN COOKING, TRY THE **ALOO DUM** — NEW POTATOES IN CASHEW BROTH — ON PAGE 97.

## HOMEMADE YOGURT

✺

MAKES 1 QUART

*1 quart milk*

*2 tablespoons plain yogurt*

Bring the milk to a boil, then let it cool to about 112°F. Whisk the yogurt into ½
cup of the cooled milk, then stir it into the remaining milk. Transfer to four
1-cup or two 1-pint jars and cover with plastic wrap. Set aside in a warm nook,
ideally between 100 and 105°F, to jell and firm up, for anywhere from 5 to 12
hours. Refrigerate, covered, for up to 1 week; it will continue to thicken.

## YOGURT CHEESE

✺

As a rule, 1 quart of yogurt yields 1 to 1½ cups yogurt cheese. Set a large strainer
or plastic yogurt draining device in a container that supports it well above the
bottom of the container. Spoon the yogurt into the strainer. Cover, refrigerate,
and allow to drain for 24 hours for soft cheese and up to 48 hours for very firm
cheese. Use as is, or refrigerate for up to 7 days.

VARIATION: As a substitute for light sour cream, add 1 teaspoon of maple syrup
and a sprinkle of salt to the yogurt before draining. (Homemade yogurt cheese has
more bite than store-bought light sour cream; the seasonings temper it.)

# RAITAS

## LITTLE YOGURT SALADS

RAITAS ARE WHISKED YOGURT SALADS, SERVED IN SMALL QUANTITIES AS A CONDIMENT FOR A MAIN MEAL. TO MAKE THE SIMPLEST KIND OF RAITA, WHISK 1 CUP OF YOGURT WITH A LIGHT-HANDED FLAVORING OF TOASTED AND CRUSHED CUMIN SEEDS, SALT, CRACKED BLACK PEPPER, AND CAYENNE OR PAPRIKA; GARNISH WITH CHOPPED CILANTRO LEAVES. THE MOST POPULAR ADDITIONS TO SIMPLE RAITA ARE: STEAMED AND DICED POTATOES, SAUTÉED CHOPPED SPINACH, SLICED CUCUMBER, DICED TOMATOES, AND SHREDDED CARROTS OR BEETS. INSTEAD, YOU MIGHT ADD SLIVERED NUTS, DICED SEASONAL FRUITS, CHOPPED DRIED FRUITS, OR BROILED EGGPLANT—IN ANY PROPORTION YOU LIKE. TO GET YOU STARTED, MAKE THE SIMPLE RAITA DESCRIBED ABOVE OR THE ONES BELOW. RAITA IS A GOOD COUNTERPOINT TO INDIAN AND WESTERN RICE, BEAN, OR GRAIN DISHES.

## MINT-CILANTRO RAITA

### SERVES 4

Combine the yogurt, herbs, and salt in a bowl; whisk until creamy. Top with pepper.

1 cup nonfat or Homemade Yogurt
  (page 34)
2 tablespoons chopped cilantro
2 tablespoons chopped fresh mint
¼ teaspoon salt
freshly ground pepper

## MANGO RAITA WITH CURRANTS

### SERVES 4

In a bowl, whisk the yogurt until smooth; fold in mango, currants, and salt. Top with cumin.

1 cup nonfat or Homemade Yogurt
  (page 34)
1 cup diced fresh mango
2 tablespoons dried currants
¼ teaspoon salt
1 teaspoon toasted, coarsely
  ground cumin

# HOMEMADE PANIR CHEESE

MAKES ABOUT 1 POUND

**P**ANIR CHEESE IS VIRTUALLY UNKNOWN IN THE WEST, BUT IT'S THE ONLY CHEESE WIDELY KNOWN IN INDIA. UNRIPENED FRESH **PANIR** IS MILD AND SWEET, LIKE FRESH MOZZARELLA, WITH A TEXTURE SOMEWHERE BETWEEN FETA AND HOOP CHEESE. UNLIKE FRESH MOZZARELLA, IT DOES NOT MELT OVER HEAT, BUT BROWNS AND BECOMES CRUSTY. **PANIR** IS AN EASILY DIGESTED SOURCE OF PROTEIN, ESPECIALLY POPULAR IN NORTHERN CUISINES. ✹ IF EVEN THE THOUGHT OF MAKING CHEESE AT HOME IS INTIMIDATING, REST ASSURED, YOU CAN MASTER **PANIR** ON THE FIRST TRY. TRY CRUMBLED, PLAIN, OR FRIED **PANIR** IN ANY DISH YOU WANT TO MAKE MORE SUBSTANTIAL — RICE, VEGETABLES, OR BEANS.

*1 gallon milk*

*⅓ to ½ cup fresh lemon juice*

Bring the milk to a boil in a large pan. Reduce the heat to low and, while gently stirring, add the lemon juice. When the milk separates into cheese curds and yellowish whey, remove the pan from the heat. Line a strainer with a triple thickness of cheesecloth 22 to 24 inches square. Using a slotted spoon, gently transfer the large pieces of *panir* to the strainer, then slowly pour the smaller bits and the whey through it. Gather the corners of the cheesecloth and tie the cheese into a tight bundle. Rinse the *panir* curds with a slow stream of water to remove the lemon taste. Gently squeeze out the excess liquid. Place the cheese on a slanted surface draining into the sink. Neatly fold the cheesecloth over the cheese to make a flat, square parcel and balance a heavy, flat weight on top of it. Drain and press the *panir* until it is firm and weighs about 1 pound; this will take at least 30 minutes and could take up to 2 hours. (For the *Panir* Cheese Torta, drain until it weighs 14 ounces.) Use as desired or wrap tightly and refrigerate for up to 3 days.

## FRIED PANIR

Cut the *panir* into ½- or ¾-inch cubes. Using a small quantity of ghee or oil, shallow-fry in a nonstick frying pan over moderate heat until the cheese is golden brown on all sides, about 5 minutes. Remove with a slotted spoon and use as desired. May be refrigerated for 1 week, or frozen for up to 1 month.

# SOURED CREAM

CALLED **MALAI**, THIS SLIGHTLY SOUR, THICKENED CREAM IS MOST OFTEN USED IN NORTH INDIAN COOKING, ADDED TO GRAVIES TO MAKE THEM THICK AND LUXURIOUS. SOMEWHERE BETWEEN THE CONSISTENCY OF CORNISH CLOTTED CREAM AND DANISH **SMETANA**, **MALAI** IS PLEASINGLY TART AND SEDUCTIVELY RICH. IN BENGAL, IT IS USED IN A FEW ANCIENT SWEET DISHES, AND ALL OVER INDIA, IN THE GRANULAR, VERY RICH FROZEN DESSERT CALLED **KULFI**. IT CAN BE USED ANYWHERE YOU MIGHT USE COMMERCIAL SOUR CREAM, WHERE YOU WANT REALLY FRESH TASTE. **MALAI** TAKES ONLY MOMENTS TO PUT TOGETHER. (TO MAKE A NONFAT SOUR CREAM SUBSTITUTE, SEE YOGURT CHEESE, PAGE 34.)

*1 cup heavy cream*
*(at least 36% butterfat)*
*1 tablespoon buttermilk*

Combine the cream and buttermilk in a glass jar. Cover and shake vigorously a few times. Set aside at room temperature until thickened; anywhere from 12 to 24 hours. Use as is, or keep refrigerated for up to a week.

# GINGERED TOMATO SAUCE

MAKES 3 TO 4 CUPS

THIS SIMPLE TOMATO SAUCE IS UNIVERSALLY GOOD SERVED OVER OR UNDER MANY FOODS, INDIAN OR NOT. ITS RICHNESS BELIES THE FACT THAT THE TOMATOES ARE BARELY COOKED. THE DEPTH OF FLAVOR COMES FROM A SLOW-ROASTED **CHONK**, A BLENDING OF TOASTED CHIPOTLE CHILIES, GINGER, FENNEL, AND GARAM MASALA. AS YOU MAKE BATCHES OF IT, VARY THE FLAVOR BY USING DIFFERENT TYPES OF FRESH OR DRIED HOT CHILIES AND SPICE SEEDS. MY THREE FAVORITE CHILIES ARE STILL CHIPOTLES, NEW MEXICOS, AND HABANERO—EITHER AS CRUSHED FLAKES OR POWDERED. INSTEAD OF WHOLE FENNEL SEEDS, TRY CUMIN OR CORIANDER.

Combine the chipotle chili or cayenne, garam masala, fennel seeds, ginger, and water in a blender and purée. Warm ½ tablespoon ghee or oil in a heavy-bottomed saucepan over low heat. Pour the spice purée into the pan and cook very slowly, stirring occasionally to prevent scorching, until the *chonk* seasonings are aromatic and a thick spice paste separates from the oil in the pan, up to 10 minutes. Raise the heat, add the tomatoes, and bring to a boil. Reduce the heat and simmer for 5 to 8 minutes. Season with salt and pepper. Serve hot, as is, or puréed until smooth. Dribble with the remaining ghee or oil and, if you like, fold in or garnish the sauce with chopped herbs.

¼ teaspoon powdered chipotle chili
    or cayenne
½ tablespoon Garam Masala
    (page 19)
1 teaspoon fennel seeds
1½ tablespoons chopped fresh ginger
¼ cup water
1 tablespoon ghee or oil, plain or flavored
1 can (28 ounces) Italian plum
    tomatoes, drained, seeded and
    crushed, or 4 cups peeled, seeded,
    diced fresh tomatoes
salt and freshly ground pepper
2 tablespoons chopped cilantro, basil,
    mint, dill, or flat-leaf parsley
    (optional)

# OVEN-DRIED TOMATOES

MAKES 24 DRIED TOMATO SLICES

HOMEMADE GARAM MASALA MAKES THESE OVEN-DRIED TOMATOES A CUT ABOVE THE REST. THE MASALA FLAVORS ARE HEIGHTENED AS THEY BLEND WITH TOMATO JUICES AND CARAMELIZED SUGAR. MAKE A DOUBLE BATCH IF YOU INTEND TO STORE THESE TOMATOES, FOR ONE BATCH WILL QUICKLY DISAPPEAR.

*8 large tomatoes*

*¼ cup Sucanat (raw cane sugar) or brown sugar*

*2 tablespoons Garam Masala (page 19)*

*1 tablespoon herb or sea salt*

*olive-oil spray*

Heat the oven to 200°F. Cut the tomatoes crosswise to yield 3 thick slices each. Place the slices on parchment-lined baking sheets. In a small bowl, mix the sugar, garam masala, and salt. Sprinkle this mixture on the tomato slices and spray them with oil. Bake the tomatoes for about 8 hours, or overnight, until they are caramelized and collapsed. They may be used warm or at room temperature, stored for 4 or 5 days in the refrigerator, or frozen.

CHAPTER TWO

STARTERS AND

SMALL MEALS

# STARTERS AND SMALL MEALS

NACKS AND NIBBLES ARE COMMON TO CUISINES ALL OVER THE WORLD, BUT IN INDIA THEY ARE A WAY OF LIFE. BECAUSE SO MANY PEOPLE LIVE AND WORK ON HER BURGEONING STREETS, INDIA'S VENDORS SELL IN-HAND MEALS TO SATISFY A WIDE VARIETY OF APPETITES. Anywhere people congregate, you'll find vendors selling enticing foods—in train stations, shopping bazaars, parks, street corners, even tea stalls near remote village wells. And each region has its favorite seasonal repertoire. Many take-out foods are wrapped in leaves or served in leaf cups and, when emptied on the spot, they're discarded. Within minutes, strolling street cows swoop down for their tasty snack. Indian streets are teeming with life and activity.

In the home, both mid-morning and late afternoon is tiffin time and quite suitable for small meals. Small meals are also eaten rather late at night, after the heat and activity of the day subsides. With the exception of Curried Popcorn (page 49) and Puffed Rice *Chidwa* (page 48), all the recipes in this chapter would work well as starters, hors d'oeuvres, or small meals, depending on the occasion, mood, and accompanying dishes.

# ROASTED EGGPLANT WITH CHAPATI CRISPS

MAKES ABOUT 2½ CUPS; SERVES 6 TO 8

**W**ITH A DISH AS OLD AS THIS, AND DIFFERENT VERSIONS ON ALMOST EVERY INDIAN TABLE, IT'S EASY TO BE INSPIRED WITH ANOTHER VERSION. CALLED **BAIGAN BHARTA**, THIS VERSION IS TYPI- CAL OF THOSE FOUND ON MANY NORTH INDIAN TABLES: ROASTED EGGPLANT, WITH ITS UNCTUOUS FLAVOR, IS FIRST SAUTÉED IN SPICE-INFUSED OIL AND THEN FOLDED INTO BRAISED TOMATOES, YOGURT, AND CILANTRO. AS IN BABA GHANOUJ, THE CLASSIC RENDERING OF EGGPLANT, THE VEGETABLE IS COOKED OVER LIVE COALS, GIVING THE DISH A SMOKY FLAVOR. ❊ TRADITIONALLY, **BHARTA** IS A SIDE- DISH VEGETABLE—ONE OF SEVERAL ON A MAIN MEAL **THALI**, BUT IT WORKS EQUALLY WELL AS A STARTER SALAD, APPETIZER, OR CENTERPIECE TO A COMPOSED VEGETABLE PLATE. HERE IT IS PAIRED WITH OVEN-BAKED CHAPATI CRISPS, CONTRASTING CREAMY AND CRUNCHY TEXTURES.

To make the chapati crisps, preheat the oven to 400°F. Stack the chapatis and cut through to make 6 wedges. Separate the wedges and place them in a single layer on baking trays. Spritz the chapati wedges with oil, and if desired, sprinkle with salt. Bake until crisp and slightly browned, about 10 minutes. Cool chapati crisps may be kept in an airtight container for up to 2 weeks.

Prepare a wood or charcoal fire and allow it to burn down to embers. With a knife, prick the eggplants in a few places and place them directly on the embers. Turn the eggplants over every 4 or 5 minutes until the flesh is charred on the outside and the inside flesh is very soft; 10 to 20 minutes. Alternately, roast the eggplants on a baking sheet in a preheated 400°F oven until tender; 30 to 45 min- utes. Transfer the eggplants to a colander to drain and cool.

Slit the eggplants and scoop the flesh into a bowl; remove the seed clusters and discard the charred skin. Using a fork, mash the flesh to a coarse pulp. Heat the ghee or oil in a nonstick skillet over moderate heat. Add the mustard and cumin seeds, partially cover, and fry until the mustard seeds pop. Drop in the asafetida and red pepper flakes and, within seconds, the tomatoes. Fry until slightly broken down, 3 or 4 minutes, then add the eggplant. Fry for an additional 4 minutes. Remove from the heat, season with salt and pepper, and fold in the yogurt or soured cream and half of the cilantro. Serve warm, at room temperature, or chil- led, garnished with the remaining cilantro and accompanied with chapati crisps.

*Chapati crisps*
*6 to 8 large Chapatis (page 27)*
*    or other flatbreads*
*olive-oil spray*
*salt, herb salt, or Orange-Chili Salt*
*    (page 22) (optional)*

*Roasted Eggplant*
*2 pounds eggplant*
*1½ tablespoons ghee or olive oil*
*½ tablespoon brown mustard seeds*
*1 teaspoon cumin seeds*
*¼ teaspoon asafetida (optional)*
*¼ teaspoon red pepper flakes*
*2 cups peeled, seeded, and finely chopped*
*    tomatoes*
*Salt and freshly ground pepper*
*1 cup plain yogurt or Soured Cream*
*    (page 38)*
*4 tablespoons chopped cilantro*

# CORN PANCAKES WITH JALAPEÑO-LIME YOGURT

✷

MAKES ABOUT 24 PANCAKES

I CAME UP WITH THIS APPETIZER WHEN CATERING FOR TWELVE HUNDRED PEOPLE AT A BANK RECEPTION IN GENEVA. THE HOST WANTED CONTEMPORARY INDIAN CUISINE, AND TO FACILITATE THAT, I TURNED SHALLOW-FRIED **PAKORA** FRITTERS INTO TWO-BITE GRIDDLE PANCAKES. WITH A FRESH CORN FLAVOR FROM BOTH PURÉED AND WHOLE KERNELS AND HEAT AND SPICE FROM JALAPEÑOS, CORIANDER SEEDS, AND GARAM MASALA, THE PANCAKES GOT RAVES FROM AN INTERNATIONAL CROWD. THIS IS A FLAVORFUL EXAMPLE OF HOW EAST MEETS WEST IN A PLEASING WAY, A GOOD LIGHT MEAL FROM MORNING TO NIGHT.

To make the garnish, combine the yogurt, chili, and zest in a bowl. Season with salt and pepper and mix well.

To make the pancake batter, combine the cornmeal, chickpea or all-purpose flour, jalapeños, sugar, coriander seeds, garam masala, salt, and 1½ cups of the corn kernels in a food processor. Add 1 cup water and process into a batter, 10 to 15 seconds. Transfer to a bowl and set aside for at least 15 minutes.

Preheat an oven to 300°F. Preheat one or two nonstick griddles over medium heat until a few drops of water dance when sprinkled on the surface. Stir the remaining 1½ cups corn kernels, baking powder, cilantro, and 2 teaspoons of ghee or oil into the batter. Brush the griddles with ghee or oil. Drop tablespoons of the batter onto the griddles. Turn when the bottom sides are golden brown, and cook on the second side, 4 to 5 minutes in all. Transfer the pancakes to a platter, loosely cover with foil, and keep warm in the oven. (Corn pancakes can be cooled, wrapped, and refrigerated for up to 24 hours. Warm in a 300°F oven before serving.)

To serve, place pancakes on a serving tray and top each one with a teaspoon of lime yogurt and a sliver of lime zest or a coriander leaf or minced bell pepper.

*Jalapeño-Lime Yogurt*
½ cup plain yogurt or Yogurt Cheese (page 34)
½ to 1 teaspoon minced jalapeño chili
1 teaspoon grated lime zest
salt and seasoned pepper to taste

*Corn Pancakes*
½ cup cornmeal
1⅓ cups chickpea or all-purpose flour
2 or 3 jalapeño chilies, coarsely chopped
3 tablespoons sugar
1 tablespoon coriander seeds
1 teaspoon garam masala
1 teaspoon salt
3 cups corn kernels
1 cup water, or as needed
1 tablespoon baking powder
3 tablespoons chopped cilantro
1 tablespoon melted ghee or corn oil
additional lime zest, cilantro, or finely minced red bell peppers for garnish

# PUFFED RICE CHIDWA

MAKES ABOUT 12 CUPS

T OWARD EVENING IN INDIA, MILLIONS FIND A GOOD SPOT TO SIT AND NIBBLE ON A BOWL OF TOASTY, LIGHT AND AIRY, SEASONED PUFFED RICE. CALLED **MURMURA**, IT'S THE EASIEST OF THE WELL-LOVED **CHIDWA** FAMILY OF SNACKS TO MAKE. THE ONLY WIDELY AVAILABLE PUFFED GRAIN IN INDIA IS BASMATI RICE, PURCHASED NOT IN HERMETICALLY SEALED BOXES BUT FROM STREET VENDORS WHO POP IT FRESH ON THE SPOT. THEY STIR A SMALL HANDFUL OF RAW RICE INTO A GIGANTIC WOK OF VERY HOT COARSE SAND, AND WITHIN MINUTES THE RICE PUFFS, LIKE POPCORN IN HOT OIL. THE SAND STRAINED OFF, IT'S READY TO NIBBLE AS IS, OR BRING HOME AND SEASON IN A POT. IT'S NEVER QUITE AS GOOD WHEN MADE AT HOME. ❈ THIS RECIPE IS ONE OF NUMEROUS WAYS TO MIX SPICES, NUTS, DRIED FRUITS, AND PUFFED RICE OR OTHER PUFFED GRAINS INTO A QUICK SNACK. YOU MAY USE ANY TYPE OF NUT AND MORE OR LESS OF ANY SEASONING OR INGREDIENT. INSTEAD OF PUFFED BASMATI RICE (OBTAINABLE FROM AN INDIAN MARKET), TRY ORGANIC PUFFED RICE, WHEAT, OR BROWN RICE FROM A NATURAL FOOD STORE OR LARGE SUPERMARKET.

*1 cup whole pecans*

*½ cup honey*

*½ teaspoon cayenne powder or
    ground chipotle chilies*

*¼ teaspoon asafetida (optional)*

*1 teaspoon ground cumin*

*1 cup chopped cilantro leaves*

*1 teaspoon turmeric or curry powder*

*1 teaspoon garam masala*

*½ cup dried currants or raisins*

*¼ cup ghee or cold-pressed peanut oil*

*2 teaspoons brown mustard seeds*

*½ tablespoon finely minced fresh ginger*

*11 cups puffed rice or other grain*

*1 teaspoon salt*

Preheat the oven to 300°F. Spread the nuts on a baking tray and bake until lightly toasted, about 10 minutes. Remove from the oven and immediately drizzle with honey and sprinkle with cayenne; toss to mix. Spread the nuts into a single layer and return to the oven for 2 to 3 minutes. Cool to room temperature and break the mixture into individual nuts.

Meanwhile, place the asafetida, cumin, cilantro, turmeric or curry powder, garam masala, and dried fruit on a plate. Warm the ghee or oil over moderate heat in a very large wok or make the *chidwa* in two batches in a large casserole. Drop in the mustard seeds and ginger and fry until the mustard seeds begin to pop. Pour the plate of spices into the pan and fry briefly until the spices are toasted but not burned. Add the puffed rice and salt and, stirring constantly, fry until the rice is slightly crisp and coated with spices; 3 or 4 minutes. Mix in the nuts. Serve warm or cool. Store in well-sealed containers for 2 to 3 weeks.

# CURRIED POPCORN

MAKES 1 LARGE BOWL

IF YOU LOVE POPCORN—PLAIN, CHEDDAR OR NACHO-FLAVORED—YOU'LL LOVE IT CURRIED. AND YOU CAN MAKE IT FRESH AT HOME USING MORE OR LESS OF ANY SEASONING OR OIL TO SUIT THE MOMENT. IN THE PAST TWENTY YEARS I'VE MAKE A GAZILLION BATCHES OF THIS POPCORN **CHIDWA**, ADJUSTING THE SPICES FOR VARIETY. THIS VARIATION HITS THE MIDDLE GROUND—A LITTLE HOT, SPICY, AND BUTTERY, BUT NOT OVERLY SO.

Combine the ginger, cumin, coriander, turmeric, curry powder, red pepper, black pepper, sugar, and salt on a small plate near the stove. Heat half of the ghee or all of the oil in a large, thick-bottomed pot over moderate heat. Add the corn, cover, and shake the pot. When you hear steady popping, remove the lid for only a second to slide in the spice mixture, and quickly cover the pot again. (Be lightning fast here, otherwise there'll be popcorn all over the stove.) Continue shaking the pan vigorously until the sound abates and the corn is popped, about 2 or 3 minutes. Discard any unpopped corn. Drizzle with the remaining 3 tablespoons of ghee or butter. Serve hot.

*3 tablespoons chopped candied ginger*
*1 teaspoon ground cumin*
*1 teaspoon ground coriander*
*1 teaspoon turmeric*
*½ teaspoon curry powder*
*½ teaspoon red pepper flakes*
*¼ teaspoon freshly ground pepper*
*1 tablespoon sugar*
*1½ teaspoons salt*
*6 tablespoons ghee, or 3 tablespoons each corn oil and melted butter*
*½ cup popping corn*

# SWEET POTATO PASTRY SPIRALS

MAKES 28 TO 30 PASTRIES; ABOUT 3 PIECES EACH FOR 8 OR 9 PEOPLE

THIS IS A VARIANT OF THE STEAMED AND PAN-FRIED SAVORY CALLED **PATRA**. TO MAKE THIS UNCLASSIC PASTRY VERSION, A GINGERY CHICKPEA FLOUR DOUGH IS ROLLED INTO A LARGE RECT-ANGLE, THINLY SPREAD WITH SPICY MASHED SWEET POTATOES, AND ROLLED INTO A LOG. CUT CROSS-WISE, EACH PASTRY REVEALS A PINWHEEL SPIRAL OF DOUGH AND POTATOES. BAKED TO A GOLDEN BROWN, THE FLAKY PASTRIES MELT IN YOUR MOUTH AND DISAPPEAR QUICKLY ON ALMOST ANY OCCA-SION. ✖ CHICKPEA FLOUR IS SOLD AS **BESAN** IN INDIAN MARKETS AND AS GARBANZO FLOUR IN HEALTH FOOD STORES.

*Pastry*

¾-inch piece fresh ginger, sliced

1¼ cups unbleached white flour

⅓ cup chickpea flour

¼ teaspoon salt

6 ounces chilled, low-fat cream cheese, cut in ½-inch dice

½ cup ghee or 1 stick cold unsalted butter, cut in ½-inch dice

sugar (optional)

*Filling*

1½ cups cooked, mashed Jewel sweet potatoes (about 1¾ pounds uncooked)

½ tablespoon garam masala

1 tablespoon minced jalapeño chili

3 tablespoons chopped cilantro or parsley

2 tablespoons orange juice concentrate or mango purée

½ teaspoon salt

To make the pastry, mince the ginger in a food processor by dropping the slices through the feed tube while the machine is running. Add the flours, salt, cream cheese, and ghee to the work bowl and process until the dough forms a ball, about 1 minute. Shape the dough into a smooth pattie about 1½ inches thick, cover with plastic wrap, and chill well. (Can be made 1 or 2 days ahead of use.)

To make the pastries, preheat the oven to 400°F. For the filling, combine the sweet potatoes, garam masala, chili, cilantro, orange juice, and salt in a bowl and mix well. On a large piece of parchment, roll the pastry into a rectangle measur-ing about 25 by 13 inches. Spread the filling evenly over the surface leaving a ½-inch border clean on one of the long sides. Brush the clean border edge with water. From the other long side, roll into a long log and gently press to seal. Score to make 28 to 30 pieces and cut crosswise with a sharp knife. Line the bak-ing trays with parchment and if desired, sprinkle with sugar. (A sprinkle of sugar on the parchment gives the pastries an enticing caramelized bottom crust, a nice contrast to the filling.) Place the pastry spirals cut-side up on the trays without touching, and slip them in the oven. Reduce the heat to 375°F and bake until lightly browned; 20 to 25 minutes. Cool slightly on the trays and transfer to wire racks. Serve warm or at room temperature. These pastries freeze well, uncooked or fully baked. If prebaked, warm for 5 minutes at 375°F.

# POTATO SAMOSAS WITH LEMON-ZESTED PASTRY

MAKES 24 SAMOSAS

I N INDIA, VEGETABLE-STUFFED SAMOSA PASTRIES MAKE SMALL MEALS THAT YOU MIGHT EAT AT
HOME, BUY FROM A STREET VENDOR, INCLUDE IN A LUNCH BOX, OR ORDER AT A RESTAURANT. DEEP-
FRIED, WITH A FLAKY CRUST, THEY ARE FILLED WITH VEGETABLES SUCH AS POTATOES, PEAS, CAULI-
FLOWER, SPINACH, CORN, EVEN DRIED FRUITS AND NUTS. IN THIS ADAPTATION OF A BENGALI CLASSIC,
THE PASTRIES ARE BAKED INSTEAD OF FRIED, FORMED INTO LOGS INSTEAD OF CONES, AND THE CRUST IS
FRAGRANT AND FLAVORFUL WITH LEMON ZEST AND LEMON OIL. TYPICAL OF SEASONINGS IN THE
REGION, THE POTATOES ARE A LITTLE HOT, SPICY, SWEET, AND TART. IF YOUR TASTE BUDS WANT MORE,
SERVE THEM WITH TAMARIND SAUCE (PAGE 77) ON THE SIDE.

*Pastry*

1⅓ *cups unbleached flour*

¼ *teaspoon salt*

½ *cup (1 stick) cold butter, cubed*

½ *tablespoon grated lemon zest*

*a few drops of lemon oil (optional)*

6 *ounces cold cream cheese, cubed*


*Stuffing*

2 *teaspoons cold-pressed peanut oil*

½ *tablespoon* ajwain *or* cumin *seeds*

¼ *to* ½ *teaspoon red pepper flakes*

½ *teaspoon curry powder*

1½ *tablespoons sugar*

3 *tablespoons lemon juice*

2⅔ *cups cooked, coarsely mashed potato*

3 *tablespoons chopped, roasted peanuts*

3 *tablespoons chopped cilantro*

*salt and freshly ground pepper*

For the pastry, combine the flour, salt, butter, lemon zest, lemon oil, and cream cheese in a food processor bowl and process until the dough forms a ball (usually less than a minute). Form the dough into 2 smooth patties, wrap them separately in plastic film, and refrigerate. (These can be made 1 or 2 days ahead of use.)

For the stuffing, warm the oil in a skillet over moderate heat. Drop in the *ajwain* or cumin seeds and red pepper flakes and fry until they darken a few shades. Add the curry powder, sugar, and lemon juice, cook for about 10 seconds, and add the potato and peanuts. Mash the potatoes to blend in the seasonings and fry for 2 or 3 minutes. Remove the pan from the heat, add the cilantro, season with salt and pepper, and mix well. Divide the potatoes into 24 portions and press each into a log about 2 inches long.

To shape the samosas: On a lightly floured surface, roll one portion of pastry into an oblong roughly 10 by 13 inches. Trim to 9½ by 12½ inches. Brush off the excess flour and cut 2 times lengthwise and 3 times crosswise to yield twelve 3-inch squares. To make each pastry, brush the edges with water. Place a portion of potatoes along one edge and roll up into a log shape. Press each seam firmly to seal and place the log, seam-side down, on a nonstick baking tray. Repeat the process to make the remaining 23 pastries.

Preheat the oven to 375°F. Bake until the samosas are lightly browned, crisp, and slightly puffed, about 25 minutes. Serve warm or at room temperature. (These freeze well, unbaked, or half-baked, ready to finish cooking.)

# CHAPATI ROLL-UP SANDWICH

MAKES 1 SANDWICH

I TASTED MY FIRST CHAPATI ROLL-UP OVER TWENTY FIVE YEARS AGO, GIVEN TO ME BY MANDARA MA, AN OLD WOMAN I SHALL NEVER FORGET. MANDARA WAS ALSO CALLED THE MILK LADY, FOR SHE TRAVELED DOOR TO DOOR WITH A LOTUS-EYED WHITE COW, MILKING HER MORNING AND EVENING ON VARIOUS DOORSTEPS. ONE DAY, MANDARA SENT WORD THAT SHE HAD BEEN IN AN ACCIDENT AND COULD NOT TRAVEL AND REQUESTED ME TO PICK THE MILK UP AT HER FAMILY'S **GAUSHALA** DAIRY. I ARRIVED AT HER THATCHED ROOF COMPOUND JUST AS SHE HAD FINISHED MAKING CHAPATIS AND CHURNING UP SOME FRESH BUTTER. OF COURSE, SHE INSISTED THAT I STAY A MOMENT, WHIPPING UP THIS SUBLIME CREATION BEFORE I COULD SAY NO. IT WAS LOVE AT FIRST BITE AND, IN MY MIND, I CALLED THE CREATION "A CHAPATI ROLL-UP." THIS ROLL-UP IS TERRIFIC WITH AN HERB TISANE ANYTIME. ✖ THINK OF HOMEMADE LEFTOVER OR STORE-BOUGHT CHAPATIS LIKE SANDWICH BREAD. LIKE MEXICAN FLOUR TORTILLAS, THEY NEED TO BE BRIEFLY FLAME-TOASTED TO MAKE THEM FLEXIBLE. THE FILLINGS ARE LIMITED ONLY BY YOUR IMAGINATION. KIDS LOVE PEANUT BUTTER AND JELLY ROLL-UPS. IF YOU MAKE ROLL-UPS WITH LOTS OF INGREDIENTS, SPREAD YOGURT CHEESE, CREAM CHEESE, HUMMUS, GUACAMOLE, OR A THICK NUT CHUTNEY OVER THE SURFACE OF THE CHAPATI BEFORE ADDING ITEMS SUCH AS FINELY SHREDDED CARROTS, THINLY SLICED TOMATOES, SHREDDED CHEESE, SLIVERED SUN-DRIED TOMATOES, AND MIXED SPROUTS. IT HELPS EVERYTHING TO STAY IN PLACE.

Rest the chapati over a gas burner set on high, or on a cookie rack resting over an electric burner on high. Warm it, turning once, until it is flexible and flecked with small char spots. Spread butter or yogurt over the surface of the chapati. Leaving a 1½-inch border at one end, sprinkle the rest with rock candy or candied ginger, cardamom, and pepper. Roll up, jelly-roll fashion, toward the buttered end, so it will seal easily.

NOTE: When making roll-ups, use thin layers of each ingredient, leaving a 2-inch, plain "buttered" border. As you roll up the chapatis, the ingredients move toward the end. Seal with toothpicks, if necessary.

*1 large Chapati (page 27)*
*whipped unsalted butter or Yogurt*
*Cheese (page 34)*
*crushed rock candy or candied ginger*
*crushed cardamom seeds*
*freshly cracked pepper*

# A CHEESE, HERB, AND FLATBREAD MEAL

�֍

SERVES 4

LIDA SAEEDIAN — A MULTITALENTED FRIEND AND GREAT COOK — INTRODUCED ME TO THIS SATISFYING IRANIAN MEAL. IT'S A FEAST OF CONTRASTING FLAVORS AND TEXTURES: CHEESE, HERB SALAD, RAW VEGETABLES, SOAKED NUTS, GOOD OLIVES, AND TOASTED FLATBREADS. BASIL, TARRAGON, AND MINT, OMNIPRESENT HERBS IN IRANIAN CUISINE, ARE ALSO TRADITIONAL SALAD INGREDIENTS. FOR SOME, A SALAD MADE ENTIRELY OF FRESH HERBS IS TOO SHARP AND INTENSE. IF THIS IS TRUE FOR YOU, TONE DOWN THE HERBS BY MIXING A SMALL QUANTITY OF THEM WITH LARGER QUANTITIES OF SALAD GREENS. LIDA USES BULGARIAN FETA ON HER TABLE, A SALTY-SOUR SHEEP MILK CHEESE. IF YOU LEAN TOWARD HER IRANIAN VERSION, FERRET OUT MIDDLE EASTERN BREADS LIKE LAVASH, **SANGUAKE,** OR PEBBLE BREAD FOR THE BREAD BASKET. �֍ FOR MY INDIAN VERSION, I PAIR FRESH **PANIR** CHEESE WITH FLAME-TOASTED CHAPATIS. I USE WHATEVER TYPE OF **PANIR** I HAVE ON HAND IN THE REFRIGERATOR — PLAIN, HERB- OR SPICE-INFUSED. FOR A COMPANY MEAL, USE THE **PANIR** CHEESE TORTA (PAGE 58) AS THE CENTERPIECE. THIS OFFERING IS MORE A FORMULA THAN A RECIPE; USE WHAT YOU LIKE AND WHAT IS IN SEASON.

¼ cup whole almonds

¼ cup walnut halves

8 ounces Panir Cheese (page 36) or imported feta cheese

salt and freshly ground pepper

fresh lime juice, preferably Key lime

extra-virgin olive oil for drizzling

4 firm ripe tomatoes, quartered, or 16 pieces Oven-Dried Tomatoes (page 40)

2 or 3 medium Belgian endives, cored and slivered lengthwise

2 banana or red bell peppers, slivered lengthwise and seeds and ribs removed

16 sprigs each watercress, tarragon, mint, basil

½ cup Kalamata or oil-cured olives

6 to 8 large chapatis or other flatbreads

Place the almonds and walnuts in separate bowls, cover with water, and soak overnight or for at least 3 hours; drain well. If using feta, rinse it in fresh water and pat dry. Slice the *panir* or feta into 12 pieces, arrange in the center of a large platter, and sprinkle with salt, pepper, lime juice, and a drizzle of olive oil. In small mounds surrounding the cheese, arrange the tomatoes, endive, peppers, watercress, herbs, olives, and nuts.

If using chapatis, flame-toast them (see page 53). Alternately, to warm flatbreads, wrap them in foil and place in a preheated 300°F oven for 10 minutes.

At serving time, if desired, sprinkle the herbs and vegetables with salt, pepper, and olive oil. Arrange the flatbreads in a large, napkin-lined basket. Diners may take a little of each ingredient on a plate and make roll-up sandwiches. The Indian approach is to break off small bits of bread, scoop up a few different ingredients, and vary each bite.

# DALPURI STUFFED WITH CARAMELIZED CABBAGE

✠

MAKES TWO 12-INCH DALPURI; 12 TO 16 WEDGES

I N NORTH INDIA, **DALPURI** IS A FAVORED STREET FOOD—A FLAKY, DEEP-FRIED PASTRY STUFFED WITH CHILI-LACED, GROUND **URAD** DAL. THIS BAKED RENDITION ISN'T AS RICH, TIME CONSUMING, OR COMPLICATED TO MAKE AS THE CLASSIC, BUT EVERY BIT AS DELICIOUS.

*Dough*

2 teaspoons active dry yeast

1 tablespoon honey

¾ cup warm water (115°F)

½ cup melted ghee or butter

½ cup yogurt

4 cups bread flour

1 teaspoon baking powder

1 teaspoon salt

*Cabbage Stuffing*

1 tablespoon oil

2 teaspoons brown mustard seeds

2 teaspoons red pepper flakes

1 tablespoon sugar

6 cups (2 pounds) shredded cabbage

¼ teaspoon turmeric

3 cups steamed mixed vegetables (corn,
    peas, lima beans, carrots, or as
    desired), coarsely mashed

1½ teaspoons sea salt

5 ounces crumbled Panir *Cheese*
    (page 36) or dry-curd cottage cheese

olive-oil spray

For the dough: combine the yeast, honey, and ¼ cup of the warm water in the work bowl of a food processor. Pulse three times and set aside, covered, for 5 to 10 minutes or until the yeast is bubbly. Meanwhile, mix the remaining water and melted ghee or butter in a bowl and whisk in the yogurt. Combine the flour, baking powder, and salt. When the yeast is ready, add the flour mixture and blend. With the machine running, pour the yogurt mixture through the feed tube and process until the dough forms a ball around the center post. (Add flour or water if the dough is too sticky or dry.) Transfer the dough to a counter and knead briefly into a smooth and elastic ball. Place the dough in an oiled bowl, cover with plastic wrap, and set it aside to rise until doubled in bulk; 1 to 2 hours.

For the stuffing: While the dough rises, warm the oil in a large, nonstick skillet over medium-high heat. Add the mustard seeds and, when they begin to pop, drop in the pepper flakes and sugar. Cook until the sugar caramelizes and turns reddish brown, then stir in the cabbage. Cook, stirring, until the cabbage is softened and dry, about 10 minutes. Add the turmeric, vegetables, and salt and cook for another 3 to 4 minutes. Remove from the heat and stir in the *panir* or cottage cheese. Cool to room temperature and divide into 2 portions.

To shape the *dalpuris*, divide the dough into 4 portions. Roll out a portion on a floured surface to make a 12-inch circle. Place on a greased baking tray, pizza tray, or screen. Spread half of the cabbage over the dough, leaving a ½-inch edge. Cover with a second portion of rolled-out dough; pinch the edges to seal well. Spray with oil. Make the second *dalpuri* with the remaining dough and filling.

Preheat the oven to 375°F. Let the *dalpuri* rise until they are slightly puffy; 10 to 15 minutes. Using a sharp knife, score in as many wedges as you wish. Bake until the crust is golden brown; 30 to 40 minutes. Transfer to a wire rack and cool for 10 minutes before cutting. Serve hot, warm, or at room temperature.

# PARATHAS—STUFFED FLATBREADS

MAKES 2 STUFFED FLATBREADS; SERVES 4 TO 6 AS AN APPETIZER

THE SMELL OF GRIDDLE-FRIED **PARATHAS** FILLS THE AIR IN OLD DELHI'S PARATHA GULLY. AFICIONADOS CONGREGATE THERE, NIBBLING **PARATHAS** RIGHT ON THE STREET WHILE THEY ARE HOT AND FRAGRANT. THOUGH CLASSIC **PARATHAS** ARE TIME CONSUMING AND A CHALLENGE TO MAKE WELL, HOME COOKS ROUTINELY TAKE THE TROUBLE TO COOK THEM BECAUSE EVERYONE LOVES THEM. THESE UNTRADITIONAL **PARATHAS** ARE MUCH LIGHTER AND ARE MADE IN MINUTES WITH CHAPATIS, BUT THEY DO TASTE ALMOST AS GOOD AS PARATHA GULLY STREET FOOD OR THOSE HOMEMADE FROM SCRATCH. USE WHATEVER YOU HAVE ON HAND BUT DO TRY **PARATHAS** STUFFED WITH SHAVINGS OF FRESH MANGO AND JALAPEÑO JACK CHEESE OR **PARATHAS** STUFFED WITH CHILI-MASHED POTATOES WITH FRIED GINGER (PAGE 134).

Warm one or two heavy, ridged or smooth griddles over moderately high heat. Cut the tomatoes into strips. Spread the cheese evenly over 2 of the chapatis and distribute the bell pepper, garam masala, sugar, red pepper flakes, and cilantro evenly over the cheese. Top with the remaining chapatis and press down lightly. Brush or spray the sandwiches with ghee or oil and place them on the heated griddle. Cook until crisp and flecked with brown spots on both sides, about 4 minutes in all. Transfer the *parathas* to a cutting board and, after cooling briefly, cut into 6 wedges, using a pizza wheel or scissors. To make many *parathas* at once, preheat the oven to 375°F. Assemble the *parathas* and bake them on trays until crisp; 4 or 5 minutes on each side.

To serve as a starter, place a whole *paratha* on a warmed dinner plate and add 2 or 3 grilled tomatoes to the plate.

NOTE: Instead of homemade chapatis, you can use ready-made organic Garden of Eatin' Whole Wheat Tortillas or Alvarado Street Bakery Sprouted Tortillas, available at natural food stores.

*8 Oven-Dried Tomatoes (page 40) or*
  *sun-dried tomatoes in oil, drained*
*4 eight-inch cooked Chapatis*
  *(page 27) or other flatbread*
*4 ounces soft Panir Cheese (page 36),*
  *Yogurt Cheese, or other semisoft*
  *cheese*
*1 cup diced bell pepper*
*1 tablespoon Gujarati Garam Masala*
  *(page 19)*
*1 tablespoon date or maple sugar*
  *(optional)*
*¼ to 1 teaspoon red pepper flakes*
*20 or so cilantro leaves*
*melted ghee or olive-oil spray for cooking*
*Udaipur Grilled Tomatoes (page 63)*
  *(optional)*

# PANIR CHEESE TORTA

SERVES 20 AS AN HORS D'OEUVRE; MAKES 4 TO 5 CUPS

THIS SAVORY CHEESE TORTA, ASSEMBLED LIKE THE BENGALI THREE-LAYERED **PANIR** FUDGE CALLED **GOURAHARI SANDESH**, CONSISTS OF CONTRASTING LAYERS OF ALMOND, GREEN HERB, AND ROSY TOMATO CHEESE. YOU NEED WELL-DRAINED, VERY FIRM **PANIR** CHEESE TO MAKE THIS DISH, OTHERWISE THE FINISHED PRODUCT WILL BE TOO SOFT. THE TORTA IS DELICIOUS WITH CRUDITÉS, CRACKERS, OR FLATBREADS. OR DICED AND ADDED TO SALADS, PLAIN RICE, OR VEGETABLES. IT IS A STUNNING CENTERPIECE FOR THE CHEESE, HERB AND FLATBREAD MEAL DESCRIBED ON PAGE 54.

*1¾ to 2 pounds well-drained* Panir
   *Cheese (made from 2 gallons of
   milk) (page 36)*
*⅔ cup blanched almonds*
*¼ teaspoon dry-roasted cumin seeds*
*⅔ cup well-drained, sun-dried tomatoes
   in oil*
*salt or herb salt, to taste*
*ground chipotle chilies or cayenne
   powder, to taste*
*1 cup cilantro or basil leaves,
   lightly packed*
*¼ cup mint leaves, lightly packed*
*olive-oil spray*

Divide the cheese and almond powder into three equal portions and place each on a separate sheet of oiled waxed paper. Place one portion of cheese and almonds in a food processor and process until smooth. Using an oiled spatula, transfer all of the cheese mixture back onto a sheet of waxed paper and set aside. Wash and dry the processor work bowl.

To make the tomato *panir*, place the cumin and sun-dried tomatoes in the work bowl and process until minced. Add the second portion of *panir* and almonds; process until smooth. Season with salt and chilies or cayenne. Using an oiled spatula, transfer all of the mixture to the second sheet of waxed paper and set it aside. Wash and dry the processor work bowl.

To make the herb *panir*, process the cilantro or basil and mint until finely minced. Add the remaining almonds and cheese and continue to process until smooth; season with salt and chilies or cayenne. Transfer to the third sheet of waxed paper.

To assemble the torta, spray your hands, a spatula, and a serving platter with olive oil. Using your hands, shape the tomato cheese into a smooth-surfaced rectangle that fits the size of the serving platter and is about 1-inch thick; square off the corners. Repeat the process with the plain cheese, making a second layer, and finish with a top layer of herb cheese. Using an oiled spatula and/or your oiled hands, pat and smooth out the sides and top of the three-layer torta. Cover with plastic wrap and refrigerate overnight or up to 4 days.

# PAKORAS—VEGETABLE FRITTERS

SERVES 6

**I**T'S THE DISTINCTIVE FLAVOR OF THE **BESAN**-FLOUR BATTER—THE FLOUR MADE FROM ROASTED WHITE OR BROWN CHICKPEAS—THAT MAKES **PAKORAS** THE MOST APPEALING OF ALL VEGETABLE FRITTERS. WHEN SLICES OF MOIST INGREDIENTS SUCH AS EGGPLANT, SUMMER SQUASH, OR **PANIR** CHEESE ARE FRIED IN A THICKISH BATTER, THE **PAKORAS** ARE SOFT AND CAKELIKE. THIN SLICES OF FIRM VEGETABLES SUCH AS CAULIFLOWER, CARROTS, WHITE RADISH, BEETS, POTATOES, YAMS, LOTUS ROOT, OR PUMPKIN COATED IN A THINNER BATTER, ARE CRISPER. SMALL LEAVES OF GREENS SUCH AS MUSTARD, TURNIP, DANDELION, KALE, COLLARDS, AND SWISS CHARD ADAPT WELL TO A VERY THIN BATTER, ENDING UP AS CRUNCHY **PAKORAS**. INSTEAD OF THE SEASONINGS LISTED, YOU CAN USE ANY OTHER WHOLE OR GROUND SPICE, HERB, OR TYPE OF CHILI; JUST BE SURE THAT THE BATTER IS FLAVORFUL AND AROMATIC. THE TYPE OF OIL YOU USE WILL GREATLY AFFECT THE FINISHED FLAVOR—GHEE, SESAME OIL, PEANUT OIL, SAFFLOWER OIL, AND EVEN MUSTARD OIL ARE A FEW POPULAR CHOICES. **PAKORAS** ARE GOOD WITH SAUCES SUCH AS TAMARIND SAUCE (PAGE 77) OR GINGERED TOMATO SAUCE (PAGE 39), STIRRED SOUR CREAM, OR SIMPLY A SPRINKLE OF LIME JUICE AND SALT.

To make the batter, combine the flour, coriander, garam masala, chilies, salt, baking powder, oil, and cilantro in a bowl and whisk with enough water to make a thickish, medium, or thin batter, depending on what you are frying.

Slice, cube, or julienne each type of vegetable in equal-sized pieces so that they will fry evenly. Pour oil to a depth of at least 2½ inches and heat to between 360 and 370°F. Dip 5 or 6 pieces of vegetable in the batter and, one at a time, slip them into the hot oil. Fry until the vegetables are tender and the batter turns golden brown, turning as necessary with a slotted spoon. Transfer the *pakoras* to paper towels to drain. Serve immediately or keep warm, uncovered, in a preheated 250°F oven for up to 30 minutes. Repeat the process for the remaining ingredients.

*1⅓ cups chickpea (garbanzo) flour*

*1 tablespoon ground coriander*

*½ tablespoon garam masala*

*½ teaspoon turmeric*

*½ teaspoon crushed red chilies*

*1 teaspoon salt*

*¼ teaspoon baking powder*

*1 tablespoon oil*

*3 tablespoons chopped cilantro*

*⅔ to 1½ cups water*

*1 to 1¼ pounds vegetables (see recipe introduction)*

*ghee or oil for deep-frying*

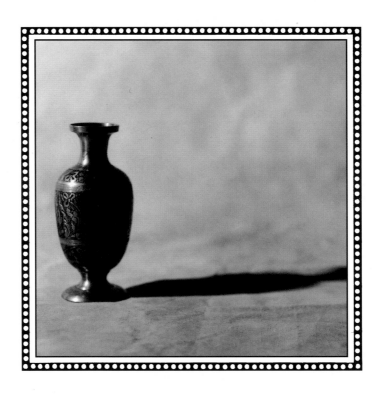

CHAPTER THREE

SALADS

# SALADS

**G**LANCING THROUGH THESE RECIPES, YOU WILL NOTE A PAUCITY OF LEAFY GREEN SALADS AND NO DOUSINGS OF VINEGAR, LARGELY BECAUSE THEY ARE RARELY USED IN INDIA. What vinaigrettes are used are not overly acidic or laden with oil, because they are made with fresh citrus juices instead of vinegar, and nuts or dried fruits instead of oil. Raitas and *kachambars*, like Roasted Okra Raita (page 71) and Beet and Carrot Slaws with Pistachios (page 70), are served in two- or three-spoon portions, like a salsa or condiment; Indian Pasta Salad (page 74), Udaipur Grilled Tomato Salad (page 63), or Curried Couscous Salad (page 67) are substantial enough to stand alone as a light summer meal.

While testing these recipes, I had access to unusual organic varieties of everyday produce and mention a few in the recipe introductions. I also obtained fine results testing the same recipes with seasonal produce from the farmers' market or supermarket. Salt and pepper are important ingredients in salad and of the many types of mined rock and sea salt tested, I prefer the clean taste of two imported salts: naturally evaporated, grayish Maldon salt from England and La Baleine white sea salt from France. Herbamare Seasoned Salt is also nice on salads. Among peppercorns, Tellicherry and Malabar from India's west coast are clear favorites.

# UDAIPUR GRILLED TOMATO SALAD

SERVES 4

FIRST VISITED UDAIPUR'S LAKE PALACE HOTEL THE YEAR IT OPENED IN 1962, AND RETURNED AGAIN IN 1995. ORIGINALLY BUILT AS A SUMMER PALACE BY THE MAHARANA JAGAT SINGH IN THE SEVENTEENTH CENTURY, IT SITS ON FOUR ACRES OF ROCK IN THE MIDDLE OF RAJASTHAN'S LAKE PICHOLA. APPEARING TO FLOAT IN THE LAKE, ITS WHITE MARBLE WALLS MIRRORED IN STILL WATERS, IT IS NOW ONE OF THE MOST LUXURIOUS HOTELS IN THE WORLD. INSIDE, THERE ARE MANY INTERIOR GARDENS, HIDDEN COURTYARDS, FOUNTAINS AND POOLS, AND SUITES FURNISHED IN A TRULY ROYAL STYLE. ❂ ON BOTH TRIPS TO THE LAKE PALACE, I SPENT CONSIDERABLE TIME TALKING SHOP WITH THE CHEFS. FROM MY LAST VISIT, I BROUGHT BACK THE RECIPE FOR THIS OUTSTANDING MIXED TOMATO SALAD, ONE OF MANY SERVED AT A LUNCHEON BUFFET. IT'S SO GOOD, YOU MIGHT EVEN MAKE A MEAL OF IT WHEN SUMMER TOMATOES ARE PLENTIFUL.

Preheat the grill. Cut the tomatoes in half and brush them with oil. Sprinkle the cumin, fennel, and sugar on the cut side, then season with salt and pepper. Grill or broil the tomatoes on each side until they are charred with marks from the grill, 3 to 4 minutes per side depending on the heat. Remove and set aside.

Heat half of the remaining oil in a large skillet. Drop in the red pepper flakes and, in a few seconds, add the greens with whatever water is clinging on the leaves. Cook over high heat, turning as necessary, until the leaves start to wilt and turn bright green; drain off the excess water and season with salt and pepper.

To serve, place the wilted greens on each of 4 dinner plates and top the greens with tomatoes. Sprinkle with sesame seeds, dribble with the remaining oil, and garnish with lemon or lime wedges.

*4 ripe, juicy, red salad tomatoes*

*2 orange, yellow, or green tomatoes*

*2 to 3 tablespoons sesame oil or virgin olive oil*

*½ tablespoon crushed cumin seeds*

*½ tablespoon crushed fennel seeds*

*2 tablespoons Sucanat or brown sugar*

*salt and freshly ground pepper*

*¼ teaspoon red pepper flakes*

*1 pound baby spinach leaves*

*1 pound baby mustard leaves*

*½ tablespoon toasted sesame seeds*

*lemon or lime wedges for garnishing*

# BIBB LETTUCE WITH CILANTRO VINAIGRETTE

SERVES 4

LETTUCE SALADS ARE UNCOMMON IN INDIA. THE HEAT IS TOO INTENSE TO GROW MANY TENDER EDIBLES, AND REFRIGERATED TRANSPORT LIMITED. IF YOU SAMPLE A GOOD GREEN SALAD THERE, IT'S LIKELY TO BE IN THE COOL NORTH AND OF GREENS FROM A PRIVATE GARDEN. ON MY LAST TRIP TO MUSSOORIE, 8,500 FEET UP IN THE GARHWAL FOOTHILLS OF THE HIMALAYAS, I PLANTED A SPRING LETTUCE GARDEN OF BIBB, FOUR SEASONS, LITTLE GEM, LOLLO ROSSA, ROUGE D'HIVER, AND MESCLUN. WITHOUT MUCH EFFORT, A VARIATION OF THIS SALAD FELL INTO PLACE ALMOST EVERY DAY. THE SAME VINAIGRETTE MAY BE MADE OF MINT OR BASIL INSTEAD OF THE CILANTRO.

*Cilantro Vinaigrette*

*2 cups trimmed cilantro, lightly packed*

*3 tablespoons chopped almonds*

*⅓ cup fresh orange juice or water*

*1 teaspoon grated lemon zest*

*¼ cup almond oil or olive oil*

*1 seeded hot green chili*

*salt and freshly ground pepper*

*4 small Bibb lettuces*

*½ cup fresh green peas, corn kernels,*
*    diced yellow peppers, or raspberries*

To make the vinaigrette, combine the cilantro, almonds, orange juice or water, lemon zest, oil, and as much chili as you prefer in a blender. Process to make a loose (fairly liquid) purée, adding sprinkles of water, as necessary. Season with salt and pepper.

Wash, trim, quarter, and pat dry whole, small heads of Bibb lettuce. Arrange each quartered head in a windmill pattern on each of 4 large salad plates. Spoon the vinaigrette into the center and over the wedges. Sprinkle either peas, corn, peppers, or raspberries around the plate as a garnish.

# CHILLED RICE, YOGURT, AND MANGO SALAD

✵

SERVES 4 TO 6

IN THE MADRAS HOUSEHOLD OF K. K. BALU, THIS SOUTH INDIAN SALAD HAS A HISTORY OF AT LEAST THREE GENERATIONS, WHICH IS NOT SURPRISING BECAUSE VARIATIONS OF IT HAVE ENDURED FOR THOUSANDS OF YEARS. CALLED **THAIR SADAM** OR **DADHYODANA**, IT IS MADE WITH FRAGRANT MANGOES, BASMATI RICE, AND THICK HOMEMADE YOGURT. INSTEAD OF MANGOES, TRY THE YOGURT AND RICE WITH COARSELY SHREDDED FRESH COCONUT, JÍCAMA, CARROT, SEEDED CUCUMBER, A DIFFERENT TYPE OF LONG GRAIN RICE, OR NONFAT YOGURT. THE SALAD HOLDS WELL, THE FLAVORS ROUNDING OUT AND IMPROVING AFTER A FEW HOURS OF CHILLING, AND IS CONSIDERED COOLING IN HOT WEATHER. WHEN YOU TASTE THIS DISH, YOU'LL KNOW WHY IT HAS PASSED THE TEST OF TIME.

*3 cups cooked basmati rice*

*2 cups plain yogurt*

*¼ teaspoon cayenne powder, or to taste*

*2 tablespoons chopped mint*

*2 tablespoons chopped cilantro or parsley*

*1½ cups diced fresh mango*

*salt and coarsely cracked pepper*

*1 tablespoon ghee or olive oil*

*2 teaspoons brown mustard seeds*

*½ tablespoon finely minced ginger*

*chopped mint and paprika or cayenne*
*    pepper for garnishing*

Combine the rice, yogurt, cayenne, mint, cilantro or parsley, and mango in a bowl and gently mix. Season with salt and pepper (I use a generous teaspoon of each).

To make the dressing, heat the ghee or oil in a small pan over moderate heat. Add the mustard seeds and ginger and fry until the mustard seeds pop, turn gray, and try to jump out of the pan. Pour the spice oil into the salad and fold to mix. Chill well or serve at room temperature, sprinkled with mint and paprika or cayenne.

# CURRIED COUSCOUS SALAD

SERVES 6

IN INDIA, I MAKE THIS MAIN-DISH SALAD WITH CRACKED WHEAT AND COLORFUL CRISP SALAD FIXINGS, AMONG THEM, FRESH WATER CHESTNUTS, LOTUS ROOT, GREEN ALMONDS, CARROTS, YARD-LONG BEANS, AND TOMATOES. TESTING THE RECIPE IN MY KITCHEN IN WASHINGTON, D.C., I USE VIRGINIA PEANUTS OR GEORGIA PECANS, AND CELERY, ZUCCHINI, CORN AND BELL PEPPERS, WHICH ARE WIDELY AVAILABLE. SEASONED LIKE THE GUJARATI DISH CALLED **POHA**, "FLAT RICE," THIS SALAD IS A LITTLE SWEET, HOT, AND SPICY. ALTHOUGH THE LONG LIST OF INGREDIENTS MAY BE INTIMIDATING, YOU WILL FIND MOST ITEMS IN THE PANTRY, AND THAT THE DISH REQUIRES VERY LITTLE TIME OR EFFORT.

Warm half of the ghee or oil in a 5-quart pan. Fry the mustard seeds until they begin to pop, then drop in the red pepper flakes and fry the seasonings until they are fragrant. Add the corn, bell peppers, zucchini, and couscous, curry powder, and garam masala and stir-fry for 1 or 2 minutes. Add the water and salt and bring the mixture to a boil. Cover and simmer until the water is absorbed; 3 or 4 minutes. Set aside.

Meanwhile, toast the nuts in a small pan until they are golden. Add the currants, maple syrup, and citrus juices. Bring the mixture to a boil, then simmer it for 1 or 2 minutes. Add the hot nut dressing, the cilantro, and the remaining oil to the couscous and toss to mix. Add more salt to taste. Serve as a main dish, with grilled vegetables or salad greens, if desired.

*2 or 3 tablespoons ghee or oil*

*1 tablespoon brown mustard seeds*

*½ teaspoon red pepper flakes, or to taste*

*2 cups (3 ears) corn kernels*

*2 cups (2 large) diced orange bell peppers*

*2 cups (3 medium) diced zucchini*

*2 cups whole wheat couscous*

*½ tablespoon curry powder*

*½ tablespoon garam masala*

*2 cups boiling water*

*1 teaspoon salt, or to taste*

*¼ cup chopped pecans or almonds*

*⅓ cup currants*

*3 tablespoons maple syrup*

*juice of 1 lime*

*juice of 1 orange*

*½ cup chopped cilantro and stems*

*grilled vegetables or torn salad greens*
  *(optional)*

# SPINACH SALAD WITH BEETS AND YOGURT CHEESE

✺

SERVES 4

TO SAY THAT SPINACH SALAD IS VERSATILE IS AN UNDERSTATEMENT; BOTH RAW AND WILTED SALADS CAN BE MADE IN MANY WAYS. I CAME UP WITH THIS WILTED SPINACH VERSION IN BOMBAY, AND DRESSED IT WITH A DATE PALM SYRUP AND **NIMBU** LIME VINAIGRETTE; IN AMERICA, I USE A MAPLE SYRUP, ORANGE, AND LIME VINAIGRETTE. THE MAPLE FLAVOR ECHOS THE NATURAL SWEETNESS OF THE ACCOMPANYING APPLES AND BEETS AND BEAUTIFULLY OFFSETS THE TARTNESS OF THE PAN-FRIED, ALMOND-CRUSTED YOGURT CHEESE CUTLETS.

Steam the whole beets until they are tender. They will take between 15 and 45 minutes, depending on size. When they are cool enough to handle, slip off the skins. Leave the baby beets whole and with an inch of stem; cut the larger ones into cubes or a thick julienne.

Mash the yogurt cheese with the salt, pepper, and semolina. Using clean, oiled hands, shape the mixture into eight 2-inch patties and coat both sides with toasted almonds; set aside. Warm the ghee or oil in a large, nonstick frying pan over medium-high heat. Fry the nut-crusted cakes on both sides until golden, for about 5 minutes. Remove with a spatula and set aside.

Place the mustard seeds in the same pan and toast until they pop. Add the spinach, apple, and pepper flakes and cook briefly, tossing the mixture, until the spinach is bright green and wilted evenly; 1 or 2 minutes. Distribute the spinach among 4 dinner plates; add 2 yogurt cheese patties to each. Add the maple syrup and citrus juice to the pan and whisk. Season with salt and pepper and add the cilantro; cook until warm through. Toss the beets in the vinaigrette to coat them and, using a slotted spoon, drain, and distribute them on the plates. Drizzle the remaining vinaigrette over the greens and yogurt cakes and serve.

VARIATION: Omit the yogurt cheese, semolina, and oil. Instead of wilting the spinach, trim, dry, and tear the leaves; combine with the nuts, apple, and 1 cup of crumbled *panir*, feta, or sharp Cheddar cheese in a salad bowl. Toast the mustard seeds and pepper flakes in a pan, add the syrup and juices and warm through. Pour the warm dressing over the salad, toss, and serve immediately.

*16 baby beets or 1 pound beets, trimmed*
*1 recipe very firm Yogurt Cheese*
  *(page 34)*
*sea salt and freshly ground pepper*
*1 or 2 tablespoons semolina*
*¼ cup sliced, toasted almonds*
*1 or 2 tablespoons ghee or olive oil*

*½ tablespoon brown mustard seeds*
*2 pounds spinach leaves*
*1 apple, cored, quartered, and*
  *thinly sliced*
*¼ teaspoon red pepper flakes*
*⅓ cup maple syrup*
*3 tablespoons lime juice*
*3 tablespoons orange juice*
*2 tablespoons minced cilantro*

# BEET AND CARROT SLAWS WITH PISTACHIOS

SERVES 6

**S**OUTHERN **KACHAMBARS** ARE SIMILAR TO MEXICAN SALSAS—ZESTY MIXTURES OF RAW VEGETABLES DRESSED IN LITTLE MORE THAN HOT CHILIES, CILANTRO, OIL, AND LIME JUICE. ONCE, WHEN COOKING A SEVENTY-FIVE-PLATE DINNER AT THE JAMES BEARD HOUSE IN NEW YORK, I PLANNED TO SERVE THIS **KACHAMBAR**. TO MY DISMAY, I FORGOT TO BRING MY MANDOLINE AND NONE WAS AVAILABLE, SO THE BEETS AND CARROTS HAD TO BE CUT BY HAND. ONE DEDICATED VOLUNTEER ENDED UP WITH HANDS STAINED CRIMSON FOR DAYS BECAUSE, FOR SEVERAL HOURS, SHE WAS CUTTING FLAWLESS, STRAW-FINE JULIENNED BEETS. BECAUSE OF HER ARTFUL HAND WITH A KNIFE, THIS SIMPLE DISH WAS ONE OF THE BEST SERVED. (I HAVE SINCE DISCOVERED THAT THE MEDIUM SHREDDING DISC OF A HAND-OPERATED, ROTARY MOULI FOOD MILL MAKES PERFECT, LONG SHREDS.) EVEN IF YOU DO NOT CARE FOR RAW BEETS, TRY THIS SALAD.

*2 cups finely julienned beets*
*2 cups finely julienned carrots*

*2 tablespoons ghee or olive oil*
*½ teaspoon brown mustard seeds*
*¼ teaspoon yellow asafetida*
*a few fresh curry leaves*
*½ small jalapeño, thinly sliced*
*juice from 1 orange*
*juice from 1 lime*
*2 tablespoons chopped cilantro*
*2 tablespoons chopped pistachios*
*salt and freshly ground pepper*

Place the beets and carrots in separate bowls. Heat the ghee or oil in a small pan. Toast the mustard seeds until they crackle. Drop in the asafetida and curry leaves. Remove from the heat, add the jalapeño, citrus juices, and chopped cilantro. Divide the vinaigrette between the 2 bowls; toss to mix. Immediately before serving, place the beets and carrots on a serving dish in 2 separate mounds. Sprinkle with the nuts and salt and pepper to taste.

# ROASTED OKRA RAITA

SERVES 6

**M**AHARASHTRAN COOKS USE CHICKPEA FLOUR TO SEASON AS WELL AS THICKEN, AS ILLUSTRATED IN THIS YOGURT SALAD. BEFORE THINLY SLICED OKRA IS OVEN ROASTED, IT IS TOSSED IN CHICKPEA FLOUR, GROUND SPICES, AND A LITTLE OIL. AS IT ROASTS, THE COATING BECOMES FLAVORFUL AND CRISP. WHEN THE CRISP OKRA IS FOLDED INTO YOGURT, IT THICKENS AND FLAVORS THE YOGURT. EVEN PEOPLE WHO ARE AMBIVALENT ABOUT RAITA OR YOGURT DISHES FIND THIS ONE APPEALING.

Preheat the oven to 450°F. Combine the okra, garam masala, cayenne or paprika, coriander, and chickpea flour in a bowl and toss to mix. Spray or drizzle with oil and toss to mix. Spread the okra in a single layer on 1 or 2 baking trays. Roast until richly browned and crisp; 15 to 20 minutes. Cool to room temperature.

Just before serving, place the yogurt and cumin in a serving bowl and mix. Season with salt and pepper. Stir in the okra mixture and half of the cilantro. Garnish with the remaining cilantro.

*1 pound okra (3 cups), trimmed and cut into ½ inch slices*

*2 teaspoons garam masala, preferably homemade (page 19)*

*½ teaspoon cayenne powder or paprika*

*½ tablespoon ground coriander*

*½ cup chickpea flour*

*olive-oil spray or oil for drizzling*

*1½ cups yogurt, stirred until smooth*

*½ tablespoon dry-roasted cumin seeds, crushed*

*salt and pepper to taste*

*2 tablespoons chopped cilantro*

# GUJARATI WILTED CABBAGE SALAD

SERVES 6

**C**ALLED **BANDGOBHI KACHAMBAR,** THIS GUJARATI SALAD IS SERVED IN SMALL PORTIONS AT ROOM TEMPERATURE AS A RELISH, OR HOT, IN VEGETABLE-SIZED PORTIONS, AS A SIDE DISH. PEANUTS ARE WIDELY USED IN GUJARAT. HERE THE TOASTED NUTS GLISTEN AMONG THE FINE SHREDS OF WILTED CABBAGE. THIS SO-SIMPLE, SO-GOOD SALAD IS SLIGHTLY HOT AND SWEET, THE CAST OF GUJARATI FLAVORS INCLUDING GINGER, CHILIES, MUSTARD SEEDS, CURRY LEAVES, SUGAR, AND LIME JUICE.

1½ pounds Savoy or green cabbage

1-inch piece fresh ginger

1 or 2 jalapeño chilies

1½ tablespoons ghee or peanut oil

2 teaspoons brown mustard seeds

10 to 15 fresh curry leaves

2 large carrots, peeled and thinly sliced

½ tablespoon sugar

1 cup peanuts, toasted

julienned zest and juice of 1 lime

2 tablespoons chopped cilantro

salt and cracked black Malabar pepper

Core and very finely shred the cabbage. Peel and cut the ginger into paper-thin matchsticks. Halve, seed, and cut the jalapeño into a thin julienne.

Heat the ghee or oil in a large skillet or wok over high heat; add the mustard seeds. When they begin to pop, add the ginger, chilies, and curry leaves and fry for about 30 seconds. Add the cabbage, carrots, and sugar. Stir-fry until the cabbage begins to wilt and turns bright green; 3 or 4 minutes. Remove from the heat and transfer to a salad bowl. Mix in the peanuts, lime zest and juice, and cilantro. Season with salt and pepper to taste.

# INDIAN PASTA SALAD

SERVES 6

THIS DISH HAS BEEN EVOLVING FOR TWENTY YEARS. IT STARTED AS CLASSIC **SEVYA UPPMA**, A NORTH INDIAN PASTA-PILAF MADE WITH VERY, VERY FINE, TOASTED INDIAN VERMICELLI AND LOTS OF SPICY VEGETABLES. TODAY, IT IS LIGHTER—MADE WITH PIECES OF BROKEN ORGANIC VERMICELLI OR UDON NOODLES ENVELOPED IN A LEMONY, SOUTH INDIAN CASHEW CHUTNEY. IT'S GOOD HOT, WARM, OR AT ROOM TEMPERATURE, IDEAL WITH SOUP OR LEAFY GREENS FOR LUNCH. FOR A FORMAL DINNER, TRY IT WITH EGGPLANT STUFFED WITH **PANIR** AND MORELS (PAGE 126–127).

1½ cups water

⅓ cup toasted cashew pieces

¼ cup lemon juice

2 tablespoons ghee or peanut oil

1 tablespoon brown mustard seeds

½ to 1 teaspoon red pepper flakes

¼ teaspoon yellow asafetida

3 tomatoes, seeded and diced

8 ounces thin green beans, stemmed

10 ounces thin vermicelli

salt and cracked or seasoned pepper
   to taste

½ cup chopped cilantro

Place the water, half of the nuts, and the lemon juice in a blender; process until smooth. Heat the ghee or oil in a large saucepan over moderate heat. Fry the mustard seeds until they begin to pop, then add the pepper flakes and asafetida. When the mustard seeds turn gray, add the tomatoes and the cashew purée; remove from the heat.

Bring a large pot of salted water to a boil; add the green beans. Break the vermicelli into 4-inch lengths. When the beans are just shy of cooked, stir in the vermicelli. Cook until the pasta is al dente, tender but firm; 2 to 4 minutes. Drain well and add the pasta to the ingredients in the saucepan. Season with salt and pepper. Stir in the remaining cilantro and garnish with the remaining cashews.

# SOUTH INDIAN CUCUMBER AND SPROUT SALAD

SERVES 4 TO 6

SIMPLE, REFRESHING AND DELICIOUS. ADD THE SPROUTS JUST BEFORE SERVING; THEY DO NOT HOLD WELL ONCE DRESSED IN OIL.

Peel, seed and dice the cucumbers. Halve the tomatoes, squeeze out the seeds, and dice. Place these ingredients in a salad bowl, add the coconut, ginger, chili, and cilantro; toss gently. (This mixture can be made 2 or 3 hours ahead to this point.)

Rinse the sprouts well, spin or pat them dry, and add them to the salad.

Heat the oil in a small pan or skillet. Add the mustard and cumin seeds, cover, and fry until the mustard seeds pop. Add the curry leaves and asafetida and sizzle a few seconds, then add to the salad; toss and serve.

1 pound cucumbers

2 firm, ripe tomatoes

¼ cup shredded fresh or dry coconut

½ teaspoon grated fresh ginger

1 jalapeño chili, seeded and thinly sliced

2 tablespoons chopped cilantro

1 cup mung bean or mixed bean sprouts

Spice-Flavored Oil

2 teaspoons oil

1 teaspoon brown mustard seeds

1 teaspoon cumin seeds

several fresh curry leaves

¼ teaspoon yellow asafetida

salt and freshly ground pepper

# POTATO AND CHICKPEA SALAD WITH TWO SAUCES

SERVES 4 TO 6

ALONG BOMBAY'S CHOWPATTI BEACH OR DELHI'S CONNAUGHT CIRCUS, YOU'LL SEE STREET VENDORS SELLING BOWL AFTER BOWL OF THIS DISH, EACH ONE A LITTLE DIFFERENT FROM THE REST. TEMPTED TO TRY LOCAL FARE, YOU SUCCUMB TO A TASTE. WASHED DOWN WITH WATER OR FRESH SUGAR-CANE JUICE AND EATEN OUT OF A DISPOSABLE LEAF CUP WITH YOUR FINGERS, EACH BITE IS VARIED, REFRESHING, AND EXCITING. INSPIRED, YOU VOW TO RECREATE THE TASTE AT HOME. ❖ CALLED **ALOO CHAAT**, IT IS OFFERED HERE AS A MAIN-DISH SALAD, ALIVE WITH FIVE TASTES — SWEET (DATES), SOUR (TAMARIND AND LIME), PUNGENT (CAYENNE AND GINGER), ASTRINGENT (CILANTRO AND CHICK-PEAS), AND SALT. IN INDIA, THE LITTLE SALAD CRACKERS CALLED **PAPRI** ARE DEEP-FRIED; THESE ONES, MADE FROM FLOUR TORTILLAS, ARE BAKED FOR TEN MINUTES. DEPENDING ON YOUR PREFERENCE, YOU CAN DRIZZLE OR SPRAY OIL ON THE SALAD, AND USE NONFAT OR REGULAR YOGURT IN THE SAUCE.

For the tamarind sauce, combine the dates or raisins, water, tamarind, ginger, and cumin in a blender and process until smooth. Season with cayenne and salt; set aside.

For the yogurt sauce, combine the yogurt, milk, and sugar in a bowl and whisk until smooth. Season with salt and cayenne; set aside.

For the tortilla crackers, heat the oven to 400°F. Using a 2-inch round cutter, stamp out circles from the flour tortillas. Place the rounds on a nonstick baking tray and brush with ghee or spray with oil. Bake for 4 minutes, turn them over, and bake them for a few more minutes, until they are slightly puffed, crisp, and golden in spots. Remove, season with salt if desired, and set aside to cool.

*Tamarind Sauce*

⅓ cup chopped dates or raisins

⅔ cup boiling water

2 teaspoons tamarind concentrate

1 teaspoon grated fresh ginger

½ teaspoon dry-roasted cumin seeds, crushed

½ teaspoon cayenne pepper, or to taste

salt or herb salt, to taste

*Yogurt Sauce*

1⅔ cups yogurt, whisked until smooth

½ cup milk

2 teaspoons sugar

salt, to taste

cayenne powder, to taste

Chaat *Salad*

*4 flour tortillas or round corn
    tortilla chips*

*ghee, olive oil, or olive-oil spray*

*2 cups cooked or canned chickpeas,
    drained*

*2 pounds (about 5 cups) waxy potatoes,
    peeled and cut into ¾-inch cubes*

*1 cup diced roasted red bell pepper*

*¼ cup chopped cilantro*

*1 teaspoon dry-roasted cumin seeds,
    crushed*

*juice of 1 lime*

*salt and freshly ground pepper*

*8 cups shredded salad greens*

For the salad, combine the chickpeas, potatoes, bell pepper, cilantro, cumin, and lime juice in a bowl. Season with salt and pepper and toss gently to mix.

To serve, divide the salad greens among 6 plates, making a circle of the greens. Nestle some of the tortilla crackers in the greens. Spoon the salad in the center of the plate; drizzle or spray olive oil on the greens and salad. Pour the yogurt and tamarind sauces over the salads and serve immediately.

NOTE: You can make all the elements of this salad several hours before serving, but make up the salad just before the meal. For added authentic flavor, sprinkle the potatoes with a spice blend called *chaat* masala or with *kala namak* (black salt). Both, along with tamarind concentrate, are sold in Indian markets.

Sometimes I use Real Salt or Herbamare Seasoned Salt, available in natural food stores.

# BEAN AND VEGETABLE SALAD WITH CASHEWS

✳

SERVES 8 TO 10

**T**HIS SUBSTANTIAL **KACHAMBAR** IS DELICIOUS ON A SUMMER BUFFET, AND IT HOLDS WELL IN THE REFRIGERATOR FOR UP TO TWO DAYS. INSTEAD OF CHICKPEAS OR BLACK BEANS, USE ANY COOKED BEAN OF YOUR CHOICE.

Combine the cucumber, tomatoes, bell peppers, corn, chickpeas (or black beans), cilantro, ginger, chilies, and lime juice in a bowl; season with salt and pepper. Heat the oil and mustard seeds in a pan and, when the seeds pop, pour the flavored oil into the salad. Chill for at least 2 hours or up to 2 days, to allow the flavors to merge. Serve chilled, garnished with cashew nuts and cilantro sprigs.

*2 cups seeded and diced cucumber*

*2 cups seeded and diced tomatoes*

*1 cup diced yellow bell pepper*

*1 cup diced red bell pepper*

*1 cup diced orange bell pepper*

*2 cups (4 large ears) raw corn kernels*

*2 cups cooked chickpeas or black beans,*
    *drained and rinsed*

*½ cup chopped cilantro*

*1 tablespoon grated fresh ginger*

*½ tablespoon minced hot chilies*

*⅓ cup lime juice*

*salt and freshly ground pepper*

*3 tablespoons olive oil*

*1 tablespoon brown mustard seeds*

*¼ cup toasted cashew bits*

*cilantro sprigs for garnishing*

CHAPTER FOUR

DALS AND

SOUPS

# DALS AND SOUPS

**F**ROM THE LOFTY HIMALAYAN PEAKS IN THE NORTH TO THE TROPICAL SHORES OF TAMIL NADU IN THE SOUTH, ONE FOOD REMAINS A CONSTANT THROUGHOUT INDIA — DAL. It's the name for any legume dish and the generic term used for any variety of dried pea, bean, or lentil. Legume soups are also called dal. From earth to table, dal is the essential protein source in the diet, eaten every day with vegetables, rice, or flatbreads. Soups, made with or without dal, are served as part of the main meal, not preceding it as a first course.

In one-burner kitchens, dal is the first thing put on the stove, because it takes the longest to cook. But not hours. The dals used in India are small, do not need to be soaked, cook quickly, and are easy to digest. While dal simmers away, rice is washed and vegetables cut. Of the hundreds of legumes cultivated worldwide, only four are extensively used in India. In the east, it's *chana* dal or Bengal *gram*, a type of small chickpea. In the north and west, mung dal is widely consumed. Throughout the south, its *toor* or *arhar* dal, the basis of a wide variety of soups called *sambar*. And elsewhere, it's black-skinned *urad* dal, eaten whole in the north with plenty of ghee, or split and husked and eaten a multitude of ways. Unfortunately, these dals are not widely available in American supermarkets, gourmet, or natural food stores. If you want to make classic cuisine, you need to buy them at Indian or Middle Eastern stores. In most recipes, an alternative dal works equally well.

# MARAWADI MIXED DALS

SERVES 6

THIS MIXED DAL DISH IS THE INSPIRATION OF MY LOTUS-EYED COOKING FRIEND, RADHIKA SARIN, WHO MAKES VERY GOOD DAL. LIKE RENDITIONS FOUND ON TABLES THROUGHOUT RAJASTHAN AND UTTAR PRADESH, ITS FLAVOR CENTERS ON EQUAL PORTIONS OF THREE GOLDEN-HUED DALS — SPLIT AND HUSKED **CHANA, TOOR,** AND MUNG DAL. THIS IS THE KIND OF INDIAN DISH YOU WANT TO MAKE REGULARLY — SIMPLE AND NUTRITIOUS, IT MAY BE SERVED WITH ALMOST ANYTHING.

Sort through the dals and remove any foreign matter. Rinse well in several changes of water; drain. Transfer to a 6-quart pressure cooker or large soup pot, add 8 cups of water to the pressure cooker (9 cups for a soup pot), and bring to a boil. Skim off the foam that collects on the surface. Add the ginger, turmeric, bay leaf, and 1 teaspoon of the ghee or oil. Cover and cook under high pressure for 25 minutes. If you are using a soup pot, reduce the heat and gently boil, almost covered, until the dals are soft and broken down; this will take 1 to 1½ hours. Season with salt. (Up to this point, the dal can be made several hours ahead.)

Heat all but 1 teaspoon of the remaining ghee or oil in a frying pan over medium-low heat. Stir in the ground coriander, tomatoes, and chilies and fry until pulpy and thick, 5 to 7 minutes. Pour a cup of cooked dal soup into the pan, toss in the cilantro, and stir to mix the ingredients. Add this mixture back into the soup and stir in the lime juice.

If necessary, warm the dal again. Ladle the soup into warm soup bowls; garnish with cilantro leaves, and drizzle in the remaining ghee or oil.

½ cup each split chana dal, toor dal, and mung dal

8 to 9 cups water

1½-inch piece fresh ginger, peeled and cut into slivers

½ teaspoon turmeric

1 bay leaf

2 or 3 tablespoons plain or flavored ghee or oil

1½ teaspoons salt, or to taste

1½ tablespoons ground coriander

2 large, vine-ripened tomatoes, diced

2 to 4 hot green chilies, seeded and cut into slivers

a handful of trimmed cilantro leaves, a few reserved for garnishing

juice from 1 lime, preferably a Key lime

# BENGALI SWEET AND SOUR CHANA DAL

❈

SERVES 6 TO 8

WANDERING THROUGH CALCUTTA'S NEIGHBORHOODS, YOU'RE LIKELY TO NOTICE THE SMELL OF THIS SOUP WAFTING THROUGH THE AIR. IT'S THE BENGALI COUNTERPART TO YELLOW SPLIT PEA SOUP, RESTORATIVE FARE MADE WITH GOLDEN **CHANA** DAL, A SMALL VARIETY OF INDIAN CHICKPEA. IN THIS VERSION, THE CREAMY SMOOTH SOUP IS LAYERED WITH FLAVORS, FIRST FROM THE TURMERIC AND GINGER SIMMERED WITH THE DAL, SECOND FROM THE ADDITION OF A CARAMELIZED SPICE-SEED OIL, AND LAST, FROM GARNISHES OF COCONUT, LEMON, AND CILANTRO. I LEARNED THIS BENGALI TECHNIQUE FOR LAYERING FLAVORS SOME TWENTY-FIVE YEARS AGO, AND HAVE APPLIED IT TO INNUMERABLE DAL POTS SINCE, RARELY USING IT IN EXACTLY THE SAME WAY TWICE. ❈ IF YOU PUT THE DAL SOUP ON THE BACK BURNER IN A PRESSURE COOKER, YOU'LL HAVE TIME TO PUT THE REST OF A SIMPLE MEAL TOGETHER WHILE THE DAL IS COOKING. FOR A TWO-DISH MEAL, YOU MIGHT ADD CURRIED EGGPLANT AND SPINACH (PAGE 135) OR CHILI-MASHED POTATOES WITH FRIED GINGER (PAGE 134).

Rinse the *chana* dal under running water, drain, and place it in a 6-quart pressure cooker or large soup pot. Add 10 cups of water to the pressure cooker (12 cups for a soup pot) and bring to a boil. Skim off the foam that collects on the surface. Add the turmeric, ginger, cayenne, and 1 teaspoon of the ghee or oil. Cover and cook under high pressure for 35 minutes for *chana* dal and 25 minutes for yellow split peas. If you are using a soup pot, reduce the heat and gently boil, almost covered, until the dal is very soft; this will take anywhere from 1½ to 2 hours. Whisk or blend the soup until it is creamy. (To this point the soup can be made several hours ahead.)

About 5 minutes before serving, warm the remaining ghee or oil in a small pot over medium heat. Add the mustard seeds and when they begin to pop, drop in the cumin seeds. When the cumin seeds darken slightly, add the asafetida and sugar and cook, stirring, until the sugar turns reddish and caramelizes. Pour the seasoning into the soup and add the coconut, citrus zest and juice, and salt. Bring the dal to a gentle boil for a few minutes.

At serving time, stir in most of the cilantro or parsley. Ladle into warm soup bowls or a soup tureen, and garnish with the remaining cilantro or parsley and a swirl of yogurt.

2 cups dried split chana *dal or yellow split peas*

10 to 12 cups water

½ teaspoon turmeric

¼ teaspoon ground ginger

¼ teaspoon cayenne powder

2 tablespoons ghee or unrefined corn oil

½ tablespoon brown mustard seeds

1 teaspoon cumin seeds

¼ teaspoon asafetida (optional)

4 or 5 tablespoons sugar

3 tablespoons shredded fresh or dried coconut

zest and juice of 1 lemon or lime

1 tablespoon salt, or to taste

⅓ cup chopped cilantro or parsley

¼ cup yogurt, stirred until smooth

# SAMBAR DAL

SERVES 6

SAMBAR, A ROBUST DISH EATEN DAILY THROUGHOUT THE SOUTH, CAN BE MADE IN ONE OF THREE WAYS: AS A VEGETABLE-LADEN BUTTERMILK SOUP, A TAMARIND SOUP, OR A DAL AND TAMARIND SOUP. IN THIS EXAMPLE, **TOOR** DAL IS SIMMERED IN A GINGERY BROTH IN ONE POT AND YAMS ARE COOKED IN A TART TAMARIND BROTH IN ANOTHER. THE DISTINCTIVE SPICE BLEND CALLED **SAMBAR** MASALA IS ADDED TO BOTH POTS. WHEN THE MIXTURES ARE COMBINED AND FINISHED OFF WITH CARAMELIZED SPICE OIL, THE AROMA OF **SAMBAR** IS IRRESISTIBLE. INSTEAD OF YAMS, USE PEELED, TRIMMED CUBES OF SWEET POTATOES, POTATOES, CARROTS, CAULIFLOWER, EGGPLANT, OR GREEN BEANS. ✺ FOR A CLASSIC SOUTH INDIAN MEAL, SERVE IT WITH, OR BEFORE, SOUTH INDIAN **DOSA** WITH POTATOES AND COCONUT CHUTNEY (PAGE 113–114).

¾ *cup* toor *dal or yellow split peas*

9 *cups water*

½ *teaspoon turmeric*

½ *tablespoon chopped fresh ginger*

2 *tablespoons* Sambar *Masala*
   *(page 21) (see Note)*

2 *tablespoons ghee or oil*

1 *pound yams, peeled*

1 *to 3 jalapeño chilies, seeded and sliced*

1 *tablespoon tamarind concentrate*
   *(see Note)*

½ *pound kale or spinach, trimmed*

1 *tomato, diced*

1 *teaspoon brown mustard seeds*

1 *teaspoon cumin seeds*

½ *teaspoon yellow asafetida*

12 *fresh curry leaves, when available*

½ *tablespoon sugar*

*salt and pepper, to taste*

Wash the *toor* dal in several changes of water until it runs clear. In a heavy saucepan, combine the dal or split peas, 5 cups of the water, turmeric, ginger, 1 tablespoon of the *sambar* masala, and 1 teaspoon of the ghee or oil. Bring the mixture to a boil, reduce the heat, cover, and simmer until the dal breaks down and is thick; 35 to 45 minutes.

Meanwhile, cut the yams into ¾-inch cubes. Warm 1 teaspoon of ghee or oil in a nonstick saucepan, add the yams and chilies and fry a few minutes. Add the remaining 4 cups water, 2 tablespoons *sambar* masala, and the tamarind concentrate. Bring to a boil, reduce the heat, and boil gently, covered, for 20 to 25 minutes.

Stack the kale or spinach leaves, slice them thinly, then chop them. When the yams are almost cooked, add the greens and tomato and cook, uncovered, for another 5 minutes or so, or until the yams are tender when pricked with a fork. Pour the vegetables and broth into the cooked dal.

To finish the dish, warm the remaining ghee or oil in a small pan. Add the mustard seeds and, when they begin to pop, add the cumin, asafetida, and curry leaves. Fry for about 30 seconds, add the sugar and, when it caramelizes and turns brown, pour the seasonings into the *sambar*; season with salt and pepper.

NOTE: Tamarind concentrate and ready-made *sambar* masala are sold at Indian grocers, though the homemade masala is far superior.

# VRINDAVAN CARROT AND MUNG DAL SOUP

SERVES 6

CREAMY MUNG DAL IS EATEN THROUGHOUT THE PUNJAB AND UTTAR PRADESH, BUT THIS VERSION IS ESPECIALLY FAVORED IN THE VRINDAVAN REGION. EASY TO DIGEST AND MAKE, IT IS MORE FRAGRANT AND FLAVORFUL THAN HOT AND SPICY, A PERFECT CHOICE FOR LUNCH WITH FAMILY OR FRIENDS. AT A RECIPE TESTING LUNCH, GUESTS LIKED THE SOUP BOTH WITH AND WITHOUT THE GARNISH OF CUMIN-FLAVORED GHEE. HUSKED, SPLIT MUNG DAL IS SOLD AT INDIAN MARKETS.

Pull a 4-hole zesting tool or a vegetable peeler lengthwise down a large carrot to scrape off shreds; collect ⅔ cup, and set aside. Cut the remaining carrots into large pieces. Wash the mung dal in a bowl, swishing the grains in several changes of water until it runs clear. Combine the dal, carrot pieces, water, coriander, ginger, turmeric, and cardamom in a large soup pot and bring to a boil. Stir and remove the froth with a slotted spoon. Cover and cook over moderate heat until the dal is broken down and soft; anywhere from 40 to 55 minutes. Purée in batches in a blender, or with an immersion blender in the soup pot, until smooth. Add the tomato and the carrot shreds and simmer for 3 or 4 minutes. Stir in the cilantro and season with salt.

Just before serving, place the cumin seeds in a small pan over moderate heat. When the seeds darken a few shades, add the ghee or butter. When it melts or begins to froth, drop in the asafetida and, after a few seconds, pour it all into the soup. If desired, garnish with a swirl of cream or stirred yogurt.

3 large carrots (about 1 pound), peeled

¾ cup split, husked mung dal

8 cups water

2 teaspoons ground coriander

1-inch piece fresh ginger, sliced

½ teaspoon turmeric

¼ teaspoon cardamom seeds, crushed

2 plum tomatoes, diced

¼ cup chopped cilantro

salt, to taste

yogurt or cream for garnishing
   (optional)


*Cumin and Asafetida-Flavored Ghee*

2 teaspoons brown mustard or
   cumin seeds

1 or 2 tablespoons ghee or butter

¼ teaspoon yellow asafetida

# PUMPKIN AND TOOR DAL BISQUE

⁜

SERVES 6

INDIAN PUMPKINS, CALLED **KADDU**, ARE SOME OF THE BEST I HAVE EVER SAMPLED. THEY ARE AS SWEET AS LITTLE SUGAR PUMPKINS, BUT GIANT-SIZED, CUT AND SOLD BY THE KILO IN VEGETABLE STANDS AND OUTDOOR BAZAARS. WHEN LIVING IN INDIA, I OFTEN COOKED IN LARGE QUANTITY, AND CAN RECALL LOADING UP A FEW BICYCLE RICKSHAWS WITH WHOLE PUMPKINS, ZIG-ZAGGING THROUGH CONGESTED STREETS, AND REACHING THE KITCHEN TO MAKE SOMETHING LIKE THIS DAL BISQUE. THOUGH UNTRADITIONAL, A SWIRL OF SWEET-ACID MANGO PURÉE IS A NICE GARNISH. IN AMERICA, I USE SUGAR PUMPKINS WHEN AVAILABLE, OR WINTER SQUASH, SUCH AS DELICATA, GOLDEN ACORN, OR BUTTERNUT. THIS IS THE KIND OF COLD SEASON DAL THAT WARMS TO THE CORE.

½ cup *toor dal or yellow split peas*

4 pounds *pumpkin or winter squash*

1 tablespoon *minced fresh ginger*

1 or 2 *jalapeño chilies, seeded and minced*

¼ teaspoon *turmeric*

¾ cup *(4 ounces) grated fresh, dry, or frozen coconut*

6½ cups *water*

2 tablespoons *ghee or unsalted butter*

2 or 3 teaspoons *salt*

1 medium *mango (12 ounces)*

½ tablespoon *cumin seeds*

20 *fresh curry leaves or 3 tablespoons chopped cilantro*

a sprinkle of *Sucanat (raw cane sugar) (optional)*

Place the dal in a 6-quart pressure cooker or a large soup pot and rinse in a few changes of water; drain. Halve, seed, quarter, and peel the pumpkin or squash. Cut it into large chunks and add it to the dal along with the ginger, jalapeño, turmeric, coconut, 6 cups of the water, and 1 teaspoon of the ghee or butter. Cover, bring to high pressure, and cook for 12 minutes, or, in the pot, bring the mixture to the boil, reduce the heat, and simmer for 30 to 40 minutes.

While the dal is cooking, peel the mango and cut the flesh from the seed. Process the fruit in a blender until smooth, then add enough of the remaining water to make a purée.

When the dal is cooked, whisk it to the consistency of a bisque. (Add more water to thin it down or boil it briefly to reduce it, as needed.) Season with salt.

To season, garnish and serve the soup, dry-roast the cumin seeds in a small pan until they darken a few shades. Add the remaining ghee or butter and curry leaves or cilantro. When warm, stir the seasoning into the soup. Ladle the hot bisque into large, shallow soup bowls, swirl the mango purée over the top, and sprinkle with Sucanat.

# CHICKPEA, POTATO, AND BLACK-PEPPER NOODLE SOUP

SERVES 6 TO 8

THIS IS A SIMPLE SOUP, INSPIRED BY ONE SAMPLED YEARS AGO AT THE HOME OF THE LATE INDIRA GANDHI. IT WILL TASTE DIFFERENT EVERY TIME YOU MAKE IT, BECAUSE SEASONAL VEGETABLE TRIMMINGS ARE ADDED TO THE POT THAT THE CHICKPEAS AND STOCK ARE MADE IN. BLACK-PEPPER NOODLES ARE NOTHING BUT RIBBONS OF BLACK PEPPER **PAPAR** — PAPER-THIN ROUNDS MADE FROM DRIED **URAD** DAL PASTE — AVAILABLE IN INDIAN MARKETS. NORTH INDIAN BLACK PEPPER **PAPAR** ARE HOT AND SPICY; SOUTH INDIAN PAPPADAMS, WHICH ARE UNSEASONED AND AVAILABLE IN MANY SUPERMARKETS, MAY BE SUBSTITUTED. ❂ IF YOU WANT TO ADD ANOTHER FLAVOR, JUST BEFORE SERVING ADD SOME SAUTÉED SHIITAKE MUSHROOMS OR, BETTER YET, WILD MORELS OR CHANTERELLES.

*1 pound potatoes, peeled and steamed*

*2 tablespoons ghee, butter, or olive oil*

*a few fresh curry leaves*

*1 small jalapeño chili, seeded and slivered*

*1 tablespoon fresh curry powder, preferably homemade (page 18)*

*8 cups chickpea stock and 2 cups cooked chickpeas, made without added vegetables*

*3 large black pepper papars or 5 plain pappadams*

*salt, to taste*

*⅓ cup chopped cilantro*

Cut the potatoes in ½-inch cubes. Warm all but 1 teaspoon of the ghee in a large soup pot over low heat. Add the curry leaves, jalapeño, curry powder, and a few tablespoons of stock. Cook for several minutes until the mixture is dry and fragrant. Add the remaining stock, chickpeas, and potatoes, raise the heat, and bring to a boil. Reduce the heat and cook gently for about 10 minutes.

Meanwhile, cut the *papar* into ribbon noodles ½-inch wide. When you are ready to serve the soup, add the noodles and half of the cilantro and simmer for about 30 seconds. Season with salt. Serve in bowls, sprinkled with cilantro and drizzled with the remaining ghee or oil.

# BENGALI VEGETABLE SOUP

✠

SERVES 4 OR 5 AS A MAIN DISH; 6 OR 7 AS A FIRST COURSE

C ALLED **SHUKTA**, THIS BITTER-FLAVORED SOUP IS AN ACQUIRED TASTE FOR SOME AND LOVE AT FIRST TASTE FOR OTHERS. THE VEGETABLE RESPONSIBLE FOR THE BITTERNESS IS APTLY CALLED BITTER MELON, AVAILABLE IN INDIAN AND ASIAN GROCERIES AND SOME SUPERMARKETS. IF YOU CAN'T FIND BITTER MELON, FRY A QUARTER OF A TEASPOON OF FENUGREEK SEEDS, ALONG WITH THE MUSTARD AND FENNEL SEEDS, FOR A MILDLY BITTER TASTE. EITHER WAY, GIVE **SHUKTA** A TRY; IT'S DELICIOUS.

Place the peppercorns, coriander, cardamom, and coconut in a blender and reduce them to a powder. Add the milk and blend until smooth; transfer to a saucepan. Add the ½ cup of cilantro and the bay leaf or curry leaves. Slowly bring the liquid to a boil, turn off the heat, and cover. Allow the milk to steep while you cut vegetables and begin the soup.

Heat 2½ tablespoons of the ghee or oil in a large nonstick pan. Fry the bitter melon slices on both sides until richly browned; set aside. Add another 1½ tablespoons of ghee or oil and warm it over high heat. When hot, add the eggplant and, stirring, fry until it is richly browned, for 4 or 5 minutes. Transfer to a plate and set aside.

Add 2 more teaspoons of ghee or oil to the remaining oil in the pan. Over moderately high heat, add the mustard seeds, fennel seeds, and pepper flakes. When the mustard seeds pop, add the potatoes and turmeric. Stir-fry until the potatoes are slightly browned, 4 to 5 minutes. Add the zucchini and continue to stir-fry for 4 or 5 minutes. Add the milk infusion, pouring it through a strainer, and the water. Bring the mixture to a boil, reduce the heat, and boil gently for about 10 minutes. Add the bell pepper, corn, and peas and continue to cook until the potatoes are tender; 10 to 15 minutes. Season with salt and pepper and garnish with the cilantro leaves.

12 peppercorns

½ tablespoon coriander seeds

¼ teaspoon cardamom seeds

⅔ cup desiccated unsweetened coconut

3 cups milk

½ cup chopped cilantro stems and leaves

1 bay leaf or 4 sprigs fresh curry leaves

4 tablespoons ghee or peanut oil

1 bitter melon, halved and sliced

1 small eggplant, cut in ½-inch dice

½ tablespoon brown mustard seeds

½ teaspoon fennel seeds

½ teaspoon dried red pepper flakes

1 pound new potatoes

¼ teaspoon turmeric

1¼ pounds zucchini

3 cups water

1 cup diced red bell pepper

1½ cups (2 large ears) raw corn kernels

1 cup fresh or frozen peas

salt and freshly ground pepper

⅓ cup chopped cilantro for garnishing

# GOLDEN BUTTERMILK SOUP

SERVES 6

SUMMER IS A GOOD TIME TO MAKE BUTTERMILK SOUP IN THE STYLE OF A SOUTH INDIAN **SAMBAR**— IT'S LIGHT, CLEAN, AND REFRESHING. DON'T BE PUT OFF BY THE LONG LIST OF INGREDIENTS (MOST ARE PANTRY SEASONINGS); THIS IS A QUICKLY MADE, TWENTY-MINUTE SOUP. TRY IT WITH RICE OR SALAD FOR A LIGHT MEAL.

1½ tablespoons ghee or peanut oil
½ cup chopped almonds
1 tablespoon coriander seeds
½ teaspoon fenugreek seeds
½ to 1 teaspoon red pepper flakes
¼ cup shredded coconut
¼ teaspoon yellow asafetida
¼-inch slice of fresh ginger
4 cups water

3 cups buttermilk
¼ teaspoon turmeric
1 teaspoon chickpea flour or cornstarch
2 teaspoons brown mustard seeds
½ teaspoon cumin seeds
10 fresh curry leaves (optional)
1 pound summer squash, diced
salt and freshly ground pepper
3 tablespoons chopped cilantro

Warm half of the ghee or oil in a saucepan over medium heat. One after another, stir in the almonds, coriander seeds, fenugreek seeds, pepper flakes, coconut, asafetida, and ginger. When the ingredients are lightly sautéed, transfer the mixture to a blender. Add 1 cup of water and blend until smooth. In a separate bowl, combine the buttermilk, turmeric, and flour or cornstarch.

Warm the remaining ghee or oil in a 5-quart, nonstick pan over high heat. Add the mustard and cumin seeds; fry until the mustard seeds pop. Add the curry leaves and squash and sauté, stirring, until tender-crisp; 3 or 4 minutes. Pour in the spice mixture and bring to a gentle boil. Add the remaining water and bring to a boil again. Add the buttermilk mixture and bring to a boil the third time. Reduce the heat to low and simmer until thickened slightly; this will take a few minutes. Season with salt and pepper, stir in half of the cilantro, and garnish with the rest.

VARIATION: Instead of summer squash, try sliced asparagus, sugar snaps, bell peppers, or spinach.

# POTATO AND SPINACH SOUP

SERVES 6

NDIAN MALABAR SPINACH, AVAILABLE IN JANUARY IN MUCH OF THE NORTH, HAS A LEMONY BITE, SOMETHING LIKE SPRING SORREL. IT IS HARVESTED WHILE STILL YOUNG AND TENDER, AND WHEN NOT USED IN THE MUCH-LOVED SPINACH DISH CALLED **SAAK**, IS ADDED TO DAL OR SOUP POTS. SIMPLE, YET REFINED, THIS TEXTURED SPINACH SOUP BURSTS WITH FLAVOR FROM CARDAMOM, CORIANDER, LEMON, AND COCONUT. YELLOW FINN OR YUKON GOLD POTATOES HAVE A CREAMY FLESH AND NICE BUTTERY FLAVOR, GOOD CHOICES FOR THE SOUP. SERVE THIS HOT IN THE WINTER OR CHILLED IN THE SUMMER.

Peel and thinly slice the potatoes. Heat 1 tablespoon of the ghee or butter in a large saucepan over moderate heat. Add the cardamom, coriander, and coconut and fry until the mixture is fragrant. Add the spinach and potatoes and cook for 2 minutes. Pour in the stock and bring to a boil. Reduce the heat and simmer until the potatoes are tender, about 25 minutes. Remove the pan from the stove and stir in the milk. In batches, purée the soup until smooth. Season with salt and pepper.

In a small pan, toast the mustard seeds, partially covered, until they pop. Remove from the heat, add the remaining 1 tablespoon ghee or butter and the lemon zest. Pour the seasoning into the soup and briefly reheat. If the soup is too thick, thin with a little more milk. To serve, ladle the soup into bowls and garnish with a sprinkle of paprika or cayenne.

6 potatoes (about 2 pounds)

2 tablespoons ghee or butter

½ teaspoon ground cardamom

1 teaspoon ground coriander

3 tablespoons shredded coconut

½ pound trimmed spinach

6 cups vegetable stock

2 cups whole milk

Salt and freshly ground pepper

½ tablespoon brown mustard seeds

½ tablespoon grated lemon zest

paprika or cayenne powder for
   garnishing

# ROASTED TOMATO RASAM

SERVES 6

**S**OUTH INDIAN **RASAM**, SERVED WITH RICE AS A LIGHT MEAL, IS THIN, BROTHY, AND PIQUANT. YOU GET THE BEST FLAVOR WHEN YOU USE IN-SEASON, FLAVORFUL, VINE-RIPENED TOMATOES; DON'T BOTHER WITH PALE, HOT-HOUSE TOMATOES. IN THE WINTER, YOUR BEST BETS ARE CANNED TOMATOES, THE ORGANIC MUIR GLEN BRAND OR ITALIAN WHOLE PLUM TOMATOES.

*3 tablespoons* toor *dal or yellow split peas, soaked in water for 3 hours, then drained*

*1 teaspoon cumin seeds*

*9 medium tomatoes (about 2½ pounds)*

*2 bulbs fennel, trimmed, cored, and quartered (about 1 pound) with 3 tablespoons fronds reserved*

*5 slices fresh ginger*

*7 cups water*

*2 tablespoons ghee or extra-virgin olive oil*

*2 tablespoons unsweetened, shredded coconut*

*1 sweet potato, peeled, thinly sliced, and cut in 1-inch squares*

*salt and freshly ground pepper*

*1 teaspoon brown mustard seeds*

*6 to 10 fresh curry leaves (optional)*

*3 tablespoons chopped cilantro*

Preheat an oven to 425°F. Combine the drained dal or split peas and cumin seeds in a blender and process until finely ground. Scatter the dal over the bottom of a large baking dish. Halve the tomatoes and place them, cut-side down, over the dal. Add the fennel and ginger; drizzle with 1 tablespoon of the ghee or oil. Pour in 3 cups of the water. Roast the tomatoes until they collapse, browned and caramelized; about 30 minutes. Do not let them burn. Scoop the tomatoes and fennel off the dal and place them in a food mill or sieve; drain any accumulated liquid into the sieve as well. Purée the vegetables, extracting as much juice and pulp as possible; discard the fibers, skins, and seeds.

Put the ground dal into the blender, add the coconut, tomato and fennel purée, and 2 more cups of water; blend until smooth and strain the purée. Pour the remaining 2 cups of water into the soup and bring to a gentle boil. Add the sweet potato, season with salt and pepper, and cook for about 10 minutes. Heat the remaining ghee or oil in a small saucepan. Add the mustard seeds, partially cover, and cook until the mustard seeds pop. Add the curry leaves and fry for a few seconds; pour this seasoning into the soup. Serve hot, garnished with cilantro and the reserved fennel fronds.

# CREAMED CAULIFLOWER SOUP

SERVES 6

ABOUT TWENTY YEARS AGO, MY COOK-IT-FAST FRIEND, VISHAKHA, THREW A SIMILAR CAULIFLOWER SOUP IN THE PRESSURE COOKER. I'VE BEEN PLAYING WITH THE RECIPE SINCE, USING IT AS A BACKDROP FOR ADDITIONS SUCH AS QUICKLY SAUTÉED, SHREDDED BEETS AND CARROTS, FRIED OKRA CROUTONS, TOASTED CASHEWS, HERB **PANIR**, STUFFED CHILIES, OR OVEN-DRIED TOMATOES (PAGE 40). IT IS A SOUL-SATISFYING SOUP THAT WILL REMOVE ANY CHILL IN THE AUTUMN AIR.

Cut the cauliflower into large florets. Combine the cauliflower, sweet potato, water, rice, coriander, turmeric, ginger, jalapeño, and most of the cilantro in a pressure cooker or soup pot. Cook at high pressure for 4 minutes, or simmer until the vegetables are tender, about 30 minutes. With an immersion blender, or in batches in a blender, purée until the mixture is smooth. Reheat the soup. Place the mustard seeds in a small pan over medium heat. When they pop and turn color, transfer them to the soup. Season with salt and pepper; mix well.

To serve, ladle the soup into shallow bowls, sprinkle with the remaining cilantro, and drizzle with ghee or oil.

*1 large cauliflower (2 pounds), trimmed*

*1 sweet potato, peeled and cubed*

*7 cups water*

*¼ cup basmati rice*

*½ tablespoon ground coriander*

*¼ teaspoon turmeric*

*1 tablespoon chopped fresh ginger*

*1 or 2 jalapeño chilies*

*¼ cup roughly chopped cilantro*

*salt and freshly ground pepper*

*½ teaspoon brown mustard seeds*

*ghee or infused oil as a garnish*

SERVES 6

**A**LOO MEANS POTATOES, AND **DUM** REFERS TO A SLOW-COOKING TECHNIQUE. WIDELY POPULAR IN THE PUNJAB AND UTTAR PRADESH, **ALOO DUM** IS A FAVORITE ON BANQUET AND WEDDING MENUS SERVING HUNDREDS. BECAUSE THIS ELEGANT DISH IMPROVES AS IT SITS, IT'S AN IDEAL CHOICE FOR ENTERTAINING AND COOKING FOR CROWDS. MADE DIFFERENTLY IN ALMOST EVERY KITCHEN, IT IS SOMETIMES CREAMY THICK AND SOMETIMES BROTHY. IN THIS VERSION, STEAMED NEW POTATOES ARE STEEPED IN AN AROMATIC CASHEW BROTH LACED WITH TOASTED FENNEL AND MUSTARD SEEDS. GREEN CHILIES WARM AND CLARIFY THE OTHER SEASONINGS. GOOD FOR ANY SPECIAL OCCASION MENU OR DINNER TONIGHT.

Steam the potatoes until just tender, peel, and cut them into 1-inch pieces. Place the cashews, chilies, and ginger in a blender and blend until finely chopped. Pour in 1 cup of water and continue to blend until smooth. Combine ⅔ cup yogurt, the turmeric, garam masala, and the remaining 4 cups water in another bowl; whisk until blended.

In a large saucepan, warm the ghee or oil over moderate heat. Add the mustard seeds and about 10 seconds later, the fennel seeds. When the mustard seeds pop, whisk in the cashew liquid. As the mixture begins to warm, whisk in the yogurt liquid. Add the potatoes and bring to a gentle boil. Reduce the heat to very low, cover with a tight lid, and let the soup steep for 25 to 30 minutes. Season with salt and pepper; stir in half of the cilantro.

To serve, ladle into 6 soup bowls, drizzle each with some of the remaining yogurt, and garnish with cilantro.

VARIATION: If you want to serve this dish as potatoes in a creamy sauce, reduce the water to 2¼ cups, and stir in 2 or 3 tablespoons of cream just before serving.

*2 pounds small new potatoes*
*½ cup cashew nuts*
*½ to 2 hot green chilies*
*½-inch piece fresh ginger*
*5 cups water*
*1 cup yogurt or Soured Cream*
  *(page 38)*
*½ teaspoon turmeric*
*1 teaspoon garam masala*
*1½ tablespoons ghee or unrefined*
  *corn oil*
*½ tablespoon brown mustard seeds*
*½ teaspoon fennel seeds*
*salt and freshly ground pepper*
*3 tablespoons chopped cilantro*

# MUSTARD-FLAVORED VEGETABLE STEW

SERVES 6

ALLED **LAPHRA**, THIS VEGETABLE STEW IS MENTIONED IN TEXTS 500 YEARS OLD, AND HAS BEEN SIMMERING ON STOVES IN BENGAL FOR MUCH LONGER THAN THAT. MUSTARD SEEDS, MUSTARD OIL, AND GREENS ARE USED IN MANY BENGALI DISHES, AND THIS ONE CALLS FOR TWO OF THEM, BUT WITHOUT THE NOSE-TINGLING FLAVOR YOU MIGHT EXPECT. GROUND MUSTARD SEEDS AND ALMONDS BOTH THICKEN AND FLAVOR THE AROMATIC BROTH, AND FINE SHREDS OF THE BRIGHT GREEN, FRILLY LEAVES ADD WONDERFUL COLOR. HOMEMADE CURRY POWDER REALLY SHOWS UP IN THIS SOUP. TRY IT WITH RICE OR FLAME-TOASTED CHAPATIS (PAGE 53).

Combine the almonds, mustard seeds, ginger, chilies, and curry powder in a blender and pulse to chop. Add 1½ cups of water and process to a very smooth purée. Warm 1 tablespoon of the ghee or oil in a thick, heavy-bottomed soup pan over very low heat. Add the mustard purée and curry leaves, if available, and fry, stirring often, until the mixture thickens and the ghee starts to ooze out; 5 to 10 minutes. Add the water and while it is coming to a boil, prepare the vegetables.

Halve the carrots lengthwise and slice them crosswise ¼-inch thick. Peel and cut the potato and yam into 1-inch cubes. Add these three vegetables to the stew and gently boil for 20 minutes. Meanwhile, seed and devein the bell peppers and cut them into 1-inch pieces. Stem the beans and cut them in half. After 20 minutes, add the peppers and beans; cook until all of the vegetables are tender; another 20 minutes or so. To finish the stew, place the remaining tablespoon of ghee or oil and the fennel seeds in a small pan. Toast the seeds until they darken a few shades, then pour the seasoning into the stew. Season with salt and pepper. Stir in the cilantro and, if desired, the yogurt or soured cream.

⅓ cup sliced almonds

4 or 5 teaspoons brown mustard seeds

½-inch slice fresh ginger

1 or 2 seeded jalapeño chilies

1 tablespoon curry powder, preferably homemade (page 18)

8½ cups water

2 tablespoons ghee or mustard or peanut oil

15 or so fresh curry leaves, if available

5 medium carrots (12 ounces)

1 large baking potato (12 ounces)

1 large yam or sweet potato (12 ounces)

1 each purple, red, and yellow bell pepper

½ pound green beans

1 teaspoon fennel seeds

3 tablespoons chopped cilantro

3 tablespoons yogurt or Soured Cream (page 38), if desired

# SURAT CORN SOUP

SERVES 6

**A**NIMISHA J. P. ARMSTRONG — A FASHION MODEL, PHOTOGRAPHER, AND LONG-TIME FRIEND — IS THE OWNER OF LE VILLE DU JAGANNATH RESTAURANT AND CATERING ESTABLISHMENT IN PARIS. THIS IS ANIMISHA'S SOOTHING VERSION OF GUJARATI CORN SOUP, AN EXCELLENT USE FOR SUMMER CORN. USE YELLOW CORN FOR ITS GOOD COLOR AND, IF POSSIBLE, WITHIN A DAY OF PICKING FOR ITS SWEETNESS.

*1½ tablespoons ghee or unrefined cold-pressed corn oil*

*1 tablespoon coriander seeds*

*1 teaspoon cumin seeds*

*1 or 2 chopped hot green chilies*

*¼ cup chopped cashew nuts*

*8 cups water or vegetable stock*

*8 ears corn, cut from the cob (3½ cups kernels), the cobs cut crosswise into ½-inch-thick rounds*

*salt and freshly ground pepper*

*1 red bell pepper, deribbed, seeded, and diced*

*3 tablespoons shredded fresh or dried coconut*

*3 tablespoons chopped cilantro*

Warm the ghee or oil in a large saucepan over moderate heat. Add the coriander, cumin, chilies, and cashews and stir-fry until fragrant and toasted. Add the liquid and corn kernels and bring to a boil. Cover and simmer for about 10 minutes.

Place the corn cobs in a second pot. In batches, reduce the cooked soup until smooth. Pass the puréed soup through a strainer resting over the second pot, pressing on the solids to extract as much liquid as possible. Season with salt and pepper and stir in the bell pepper and coconut. Simmer for 5 minutes or until the corn cobs and soup are piping hot. Garnish with cilantro.

CHAPTER FIVE

ENTRÉES

# ENTRÉES: GRAIN, BEAN, AND PANIR DISHES

✹

THIS CHAPTER HOUSES SOME OF INDIA'S MOST ENDURING DISHES, SOME THAT MAY END UP ON YOUR LIST OF FAVORITES. If specialties such as *kitcheree, kofta, dosa,* and *uppma* are new to your lexicon, you're in for a treat, because they are as enjoyable to make as they are to eat. If you serve a vegetarian meal in courses or want a composed plate with a centerpiece, these dishes make good entrées for an Indian or mixed cuisine menu. In smaller portions they can be worked into traditional Indian-style service.

An Indian meal is not served in courses, but all at once, on a large plate called a *thali.* Made of stainless steel, bell metal, silver, and even gold, the *thali* ranges from eight to twenty inches in diameter. Liquid dishes are served in small bowls, called *katoris* and made of the same material, that are placed directly on the *thali.* A good alternative is the use of a restaurant-sized white porcelain or china plate, between twelve and fourteen inches around. Like a *thali,* it is large enough to accommodate small portions of several dishes, and like metal, the white backdrop makes food look good. Porcelain plates are reasonably priced in mail-order catalogues, outlet malls, and restaurant supply stores. White china plates of a similar size are often called serving platters, and cost five or six times more. Instead of metal *katoris,* use small matching bowls placed around the top edge of the plate.

In some of the recipe introductions, I suggest a few accompanying dishes to make a meal. You can always build upon this for more elaborate menus. By Western standards, an ordinary Indian lunch seems like a banquet because it includes tastes of eight dishes or more, including a dal dish, rice and/or chapatis, two or three different vegetable dishes of different textures, a few spoons of yogurt *raita* salad, a raw *kachambar* vegetable salad, and a taste of palate-teasing fresh chutney. If you want to try this, select other dishes from the book or peruse the basics chapter and devise a seasonal menu just right for the occasion.

# BROWN RICE AND MUNG BEAN KITCHEREE

SERVES 6 HEARTY APPETITES

KITCHEREE, RELISHED IN MANY INDIAN HOMES EVERY DAY, IS ABOUT AS CLOSE TO INDIAN SOUL FOOD AS IT GETS. THOUGH HIGHLY REVERED IN INDIA, IT IS JUST ABOUT UNKNOWN ELSEWHERE, AND THAT'S A SHAME. THIS IS A TOOTHSOME **KITCHEREE**, RICHLY TEXTURED WITH BROWN RICE, WHOLE MUNG BEANS, AND VEGETABLES. MADE IN A PRESSURE COOKER, IT'S A ONE-POT, ONE-DISH MEAL DONE IN RECORD TIME, ALTHOUGH IT WILL TAKE AN HOUR SIMMERED ON THE STOVE. DON'T FEEL LIMITED TO THE VEGETABLES LISTED; I USE WHATEVER IS IN SEASON, AND RARELY THE SAME COMBINATION TWICE.

*1¼ cups whole mung beans*
*1½ cups long-grain brown rice*
*2 tablespoons unrefined corn oil*
*1½ tablespoons grated fresh ginger*
*½ teaspoon crushed red pepper flakes*
*1 tablespoon brown mustard seeds*
*2 teaspoons cumin seeds*
*1 teaspoon turmeric*
*1 pound carrots, cut ½-inch thick*
*1 cup shelled, fresh fava beans or lima beans*
*8 cups hot water*
*2 ears corn*
*1 pound fresh spinach, stemmed and chopped*
*1 cup shucked green peas*
*2 ripe tomatoes, cut in eighths*
*¼ cup chopped cilantro*
*salt and freshly ground pepper*

Sort through the mung beans and rice and remove any foreign matter. Combine both in a large bowl and rinse several times with clean water, swishing the grains, until the water runs clear; drain in a strainer. Warm the oil in a 6-quart pressure cooker or a nonstick or heavy-bottomed, 5-quart saucepan over moderate heat. Add the ginger, pepper flakes, mustard seeds, and cumin and fry until the mustard seeds pop. Add the mung beans and rice, turmeric, carrots, and fresh beans. If you are using a pressure cooker, add 6 cups of water and bring to a boil. Cook for 9 minutes at high pressure. If you are using a saucepan, add all 8 cups of the liquid at once, and bring to a boil. Cook over medium-low heat, partially covered and stirring occasionally, until about 5 minutes short of serving; almost 1 hour.

Shuck the corn, and cut the cobs crosswise into rounds ½-inch thick. Add the peas, corn, spinach, tomatoes, half of the cilantro, and, to the pressure cooker, the remaining 2 cups water. Mix gently. Place the pan over moderate heat and cook for 4 or 5 minutes, or enough time to allow the grains to absorb the liquid and the vegetables to cook briefly. Season with salt and pepper. At serving time, garnish with the remaining cilantro.

# MUNG AND CAULIFLOWER KITCHEREE

SERVES 6 TO 8

ELEGANT IN ITS SIMPLICITY, **KITCHEREE** IS AS POPULAR IN INDIA AS RISOTTO IS IN ITALY. IT'S NOT THE WAY IN WHICH THIS **KITCHEREE** IS COOKED, BUT RATHER ITS FINISHED TEXTURE THAT SO RESEMBLES RICH, SUCCULENT **RISOTTO**. THE DISH TAKES ONLY SIX MINUTES IN A PRESSURE COOKER, AND ABOUT FORTY-FIVE MINUTES ON THE STOVETOP, MAKING IT AN IDEAL WEEKDAY DINNER. AT SERVING TIME, **KITCHEREE** IS DRIZZLED WITH GHEE, NOT ONLY FOR TASTE, BUT TO AID IN ASSIMILATING ITS GOODNESS. YOU MAY USE A LITTLE OR A LOT, OR JUST A FEW DROPS. IT IS ALSO DELICIOUS SPRINKLED, UNTRADITIONALLY, WITH GRATED, DRY MONTEREY JACK CHEESE.

¾ cup split, husked mung dal

1¾ cups basmati rice

½ tablespoon cumin seeds

1½ tablespoons grated fresh ginger

1 or 2 teaspoons crushed red pepper
    flakes

3 cardamom pods, crushed

½ teaspoon turmeric

¼ teaspoon yellow asafetida

4 tablespoons ghee, or 2 tablespoons
    each corn oil and butter

1 cauliflower, trimmed and cut in florets

7½ cups hot water or vegetable stock

2 cups chopped tomatoes or baby peas

½ cup chopped cilantro

salt and coarsely ground pepper

Sort through the dal and rice and remove any foreign matter. Transfer to a large bowl and rinse several times with clean changes of water, swishing the grains until the water is clear; drain in a strainer.

Place the cumin, ginger, red pepper flakes, cardamom, turmeric, and asafetida in piles on a plate. Heat 3 tablespoons of ghee or oil in a pressure cooker or in a nonstick or heavy-bottomed, 5-quart saucepan over medium-high heat. Add the cumin, ginger, pepper flakes, cardamom pods, and, when the cumin turns medium brown, the turmeric and asafetida. Within 5 seconds, add the cauliflower, rice, and dal. Cook, stirring, for 2 minutes.

If you are using a pressure cooker, pour in 5½ cups of the water or stock and bring to a boil. Cook at high pressure for 6 minutes. Off the heat, pour in the remaining 2 cups liquid, the tomatoes or peas, and ¼ cup cilantro. Season with salt and pepper and mix gently. Place the pan over moderate heat for 1 or 2 minutes to allow the grains to absorb the liquid and warm the tomatoes or peas.

If you are using a saucepan, add all 7 cups of the liquid at once. Bring to a boil. Cook over low heat, partially covered and stirring occasionally, for 40 to 60 minutes, or until the rice is tender, the dal is soft or breaking down, and the liquid is absorbed.

At serving time, garnish with the remaining cilantro and dribble with the remaining ghee or butter.

# SAFFRON BASMATI RICE WITH LENTILS AND CRANBERRY CHUTNEY

SERVES 6

THIS IS AN INDIAN VERSION OF THE MEDIEVAL IRANIAN DISH CALLED **ADAS PULAU**, SO EXPERTLY MADE BY MY FRIEND, LIDA SAEEDIAN. IT'S A LAYERED DISH OF CONTRASTING TEXTURES, FLAVORS, AND COLORS—PLAIN AND SAFFRON BASMATI RICE, PLUMP BROWN LENTILS, AND SWEET RED CHUTNEY. THE CLASSIC INGREDIENT FOR THIS CHUTNEY IS A SOUR, DRIED BERRY CALLED **ZERESHK**. THEY LOOK LIKE LITTLE FACETED RUBIES AND ARE AVAILABLE AT MIDDLE EASTERN GROCERS. FOR CONVENIENCE, I PREFER MAKING THE CHUTNEY WITH DRIED CRANBERRIES AND CURRANTS. I HAVE MADE THE DISH WITH INDIAN **MUTH** DAL LENTILS, EGYPTIAN LENTILS, THE SPECIAL FRENCH **LENTILLES DE PUY,** AND SUPERMARKET BROWN LENTILS; YOUR PREFERENCES WILL DEPEND ON YOUR TASTES. ❁ FOR A **THALI** MEAL OR COMPOSED PLATE, SERVE THE ELEGANT RICE WITH SMALL PORTIONS OF TWO OR THREE VEGETABLE DISHES.

1½ cups basmati rice

2 tablespoons salt

1 teaspoon cumin seeds, crushed

1 cup green or brown lentils

5 tablespoons ghee or corn oil

⅓ cup dried currants

⅛ teaspoon turmeric

*Cranberry Chutney*

⅓ teaspoon fine saffron threads

½ cup dried cranberries or zereshk

1¼ cups water

¼ cup fructose or sugar

2 teaspoons ghee or good corn oil

In a bowl, swish the rice in several changes of water until it runs clear; drain. Dissolve 1½ tablespoons of the salt in 3 cups of water, add the rice, and set aside to soak for at least 2 hours; drain. Bring a large pot of water to a boil, stir in the rice, and cook it until it is just over half cooked, about 3 or 4 minutes. Pour the rice into a colander and rinse it for a few seconds under warm water; drain, and set aside, covered. Toast the cumin in a saucepan until it is fragrant. Add the lentils, 1 cup of water, 1 teaspoon ghee or oil, and the remaining salt; bring to a boil. Reduce the heat and simmer, covered, just until the lentils are plump and tender; 15 to 20 minutes. Drain off any excess liquid.

To make the chutney, powder the saffron threads in a small mortar and pestle and set it aside. If using dried cranberries, chop them in a food processor until they are the size of whole peppercorns; set aside. (*Zereshk* need not be chopped.) Combine the water, the fructose or sugar, the ghee or oil, and the powdered saffron in a small pot and bring the mixture to a boil over moderate heat. Add the cranberries or *zereshk* and currants. Cook 1 to 3 minutes, or until the fruit is plump; set aside.

To assemble the *pulau*, warm 2 teaspoons of ghee or oil in a heavy-bottomed or nonstick, 5-quart pan over medium heat. Add the remaining saffron powder, the turmeric, and 3 tablespoons of water to the pot. Add ¾ cup of the half-cooked rice, and gently mix to make brightly colored saffron rice; remove and set aside. To the same pan, add 2 tablespoons of ghee or oil, and strew 1 cup of the half-cooked rice over the bottom of it. Cover with about ¾ cup lentils, and finish layering the remaining rice and lentils. Cover and cook for about 3 minutes. Sprinkle with the remaining water and 2 tablespoons of ghee or oil. Cover the pan with a piece of kitchen parchment, heavy aluminum foil, or a dampened kitchen towel, and a tight-fitting lid. Turn the heat to its lowest setting and cook for about 45 minutes.

To serve, fill the kitchen sink with cold water to the depth of 3 inches. Set the covered rice pot in the water for 2 or 3 minutes to loosen the bottom crust. Using a large serving spatula, and stopping just short of the crisp crust on the bottom, transfer portions of the layered dish to a warmed serving platter. Sprinkle the brightly-colored saffron rice over the top. On the diagonal, spoon 2 or 3 lines of chutney across the top. Dribble with an additional teaspoon ghee or oil. (If desired, break up the golden crust and scatter it around the edges of the platter; some consider this a delicacy and the best part.)

# MUSSOORIE MUNG BEANS WITH VEGETABLES

SERVES 6

**N**ORTH INDIAN WHOLE MUNG AND **URAD** BEAN DISHES ARE OFTEN EXCEEDINGLY RICH—ALMOST FLOATING IN GHEE AND FINISHED OFF WITH HOMEMADE BUTTER. WITH A RICH TASTE, AND FAR LESS FAT, HERE IS AN ADAPTATION OF A DISH MADE BY A TEN-YEAR-OLD GIRL. I STUMBLED UPON HER NEAR A PATH JUST OUTSIDE MUSSOORIE, IN THE HIMALAYAN FOOTHILLS. ASSISTED ONLY BY HER SEVEN-YEAR-OLD BROTHER, HER PARENTS FAR AWAY IN THE FIELDS, SHE ADEPTLY AND SIMULTANEOUSLY TENDED A FIRE, COOKED MUNG BEANS WITH MAUVE-TINGED TURNIPS, MADE BUTTER, AND TENDED COWS, SMILING ALL THE WHILE. I ADMIRED HER CREATIVITY AND COMPETENCE FOR AN ENTIRE MORNING. THIS DISH BECKONS THE CREATIVE INSTINCTS AND IS EXCELLENT WITH VIRTUALLY ANY COMBINATION OF SAUTÉED OR BAKED SEASONAL VEGETABLES.

1⅓ cup whole mung beans

¼ teaspoon turmeric

5 cups water

2 or 3 tablespoons ghee or corn oil

1½ pounds trimmed spinach leaves or
    other greens

1½ cups Gingered Tomato Sauce
    (page 39)

*Late-Winter Vegetables*

1 tablespoon grated fresh ginger

1 or 2 pinches crushed red pepper flakes

2 cups thinly sliced carrots

2 cups thinly sliced turnips or parsnips

2 cups cooked, coarsely mashed potatoes

salt and freshly ground pepper

3 tablespoons chopped cilantro and
    sprigs for garnish

lemon wedges

Sort through the beans and remove any shriveled kernels and foreign matter; rinse in a colander. Place the beans, turmeric, water and ½ tablespoon of the ghee or oil in a heavy saucepan; bring to a boil. Reduce the heat and gently cook, partially covered, until the beans are just tender, but not broken down, 1 to 1½ hours. Add water as necessary or drain off excess liquid. Reduce to the lowest heat, add the spinach or greens and tomato sauce and cover. (Can be made to this point many hours before serving; gently reheat when needed.)

About 10 minutes before serving, heat all but 2 teaspoons of the remaining ghee or oil in a nonstick sauté pan or wok over high heat. Add the ginger and red pepper flakes and sizzle for about 15 seconds. Stir in the carrots and turnips or parsnips and sauté them for 2 or 3 minutes. Reduce the heat to medium and cover. Cook until the vegetables are just tender and add them to the beans, along with the potatoes. Season with salt and pepper and, when everything is piping hot, fold in the cilantro. Garnish with cilantro sprigs and lemon wedges, and dribble with the remaining ghee or oil.

# BLACK-EYED PEAS WITH ROASTED PEPPERS

SERVES 6 TO 8

ON THE WEST COAST OF INDIA, ESPECIALLY IN GUJARAT, MANY COOKS FAVOR BLACK-EYED PEAS. THREE HERBS ARE ROUTINELY ADDED TO BLACK-EYED PEA DISHES: FRESH DILL, CILANTRO, OR CURRY LEAVES. ANY ONE OF THEM WOULD BE GOOD IN THIS DISH. CALLED **LOBHIYA**, THIS IS A WESTERN EQUIVALENT OF THE NORTHERN RED BEAN CHILI, HEARTY AND WARMING, THE ROASTED BELL PEPPERS GIVING IT ADDITIONAL COLOR AND FLAVOR. SERVE THIS SIMPLE AND GOOD DISH WITH SURAT CORN SOUP (PAGE 100) IN THE SUMMER AND RICE IN THE WINTER.

*2½ cups (1 pound) dried black-eyed peas*
*4 or 5 cups water, or as needed*
*2 bay leaves*
*1 tablespoon minced fresh ginger*
*¼ teaspoon turmeric*
*2½ tablespoons ghee or corn oil*
*3 yellow and 3 orange bell peppers (3 pounds)*

*Gujarati Masala and Tomato Garnish*
*2 teaspoons brown mustard seeds*
*2 teaspoons cumin seeds*
*½ tablespoon fennel seeds*
*½ to 1 teaspoon crushed red pepper flakes*
*¼ teaspoon yellow asafetida*
*2 cups chopped tomatoes, fresh or canned*
*⅔ cup chopped cilantro or dill, or about 20 curry leaves*
*salt and freshly ground pepper*

Place the black-eyed peas in a large saucepan, rinse well, and drain them. Place the pan on high heat, add 5 cups of water, the bay leaves, ginger, turmeric and ½ tablespoon of the ghee or oil. Bring to a boil, reduce the heat, cover, and gently boil until the beans are soft, 45 minutes to 1 hour. Add more liquid if necessary. (Alternately, place the drained peas in a large pressure cooker with 4 cups of water and the flavorings. Cover and bring to high pressure; cook 10 to 12 minutes. If the peas are not soft, place the cooker over heat and gently boil until they are tender, adding more water if necessary.)

Meanwhile, preheat the broiler. Stem, halve, seed, and devein the bell peppers. Place them cut-side down on a baking tray. Broil until the skins are well blackened, 5 to 8 minutes. Cool, then slip off the skins. Cut each half crosswise, and then cut into strips about ½-inch wide; set aside. When the beans are tender, drain off and reserve the excess liquid.

To finish the dish, warm the 2 tablespoons remaining ghee or oil in a nonstick skillet over medium-high heat. Add the mustard seeds, and when they begin to pop, drop in the cumin seeds, fennel seeds, and pepper flakes. Fry until the cumin seeds darken a few shades, then sprinkle in the asafetida. Within 5 seconds add the tomatoes and most of the cilantro or dill, or all of the curry leaves. Stir-fry for 2 or 3 minutes, then pour the mixture into the cooked beans. At this point, add the roasted peppers and as much cooking liquid or water as you like, up to 1½ cups. Season with salt and pepper, gently mix, and warm through over moderate heat. Serve in individual bowls, garnished with the remaining herbs.

# SOUTH INDIAN DOSA WITH POTATOES AND COCONUT CHUTNEY

❉

SERVES 6

A FEW DISHES ARE EATEN EVERY DAY IN THE SOUTHERN STATES OF KARNATAKA, ANDHRA PRADESH, KERALA, AND TAMIL NADU, AND **DOSA** IS ONE OF THEM. LIKE PASTA IN ITALY, IT IS RELISHED MANY WAYS. THIS ONE IS CALLED MASALA **DOSA**—EGGLESS CRÊPELIKE PANCAKES THAT ARE WRAPPED AROUND SEASONED MASHED POTATOES AND SERVED WITH A MOIST COCONUT CHUTNEY. SERVE THIS DISH AS A LIGHT MEAL BY ITSELF WITH RICE ANYTIME, OR AS AN ENTRÉE PRECEDED BY **SAMBAR** DAL (PAGE 86) AND SALAD.

Combine the cornmeal, semolina, pastry flour, cumin, pepper flakes, and cilantro with 3 cups of water in a mixing bowl; mix well. Cover and set aside for at least 2 hours or overnight. When you are ready to make the *dosa*, add enough of the remaining water to make a pourable, thinnish, crêpelike batter. Stir in the salt, soda, and ½ tablespoon of the oil.

Heat 2 or 3 large, nonstick omelet pans or griddles over medium to medium-high heat. Stir the batter between each use. To make each *dosa*, scoop out ½ cup of batter and pour it over the bottom of a pan. Lift and tilt the pan so the batter flows to make an 8- to 9-inch crêpe. Cook until the edges begin to curl and the bottom turns golden brown, 3 to 4 minutes. Flip over and cook on the second side. Stack the *dosa* browned-side down. (The *dosa* may be made 2 days ahead of use; to store, refrigerate them, well sealed.)

To make the filling, place the corn in a frying pan with a few spoons of water and steam it for a few minutes. Add the potatoes, season with salt and pepper, and mix well. With the browned side of the *dosa* down, spoon some potato filling down the center of each crêpe. Roll up to enclose the filling and transfer the *dosa* to a shallow, oiled baking tray.

To make the chutney, whisk the coconut and yogurt in a bowl. Fry the oil, mustard seeds, chilies and dal in a small pan until the dal turns brown and the mustard seeds crackle and pop. Add the asafetida and curry leaves and let them sizzle for about 10 seconds. Pour the seasoning into the yogurt and stir to mix.

## Dosa

1 cup stone-ground cornmeal

1 cup semolina

1 cup whole wheat pastry flour

2 teaspoons cumin seeds

½ tablespoon crushed red pepper flakes

3 tablespoons chopped cilantro

1 cup yogurt

3 to 3½ cups water

1 teaspoon salt

pinch of baking soda

unrefined corn oil for cooking, as needed

1 cup corn kernels

1 recipe Chili-Mashed Potatoes with
    Fried Ginger (page 134)

salt and freshly ground pepper

*Coconut Chutney*

*1 cup grated fresh or dried coconut*

*2 cups yogurt*

*2 teaspoons unrefined corn oil*

*1 teaspoon brown mustard seeds*

*1 large jalapeño chili, seeded and slivered*

*1 teaspoon split* urad *dal (optional)*

*¼ teaspoon yellow asafetida*

*15 fresh curry leaves*

Just before serving, cover and bake the *dosa* in a preheated 375°F oven for about 15 minutes. As an entrée, serve 2 *dosa* per person, with chutney.

NOTE: This recipe makes at least twelve 8½-inch *dosa* or eighteen 6½-inch *dosa*. To make 8½-inch *dosa* for an entrée, use ½-cup quantities of batter. To make smaller *dosa*, use a smaller pan and between ¼- and ⅓-cup amounts of batter. If your nonstick surface is old, you may need to drizzle a few drops of oil around the *dosa* as it cooks.

# VEGETABLE KOFTAS

SERVES 4 TO 6

**D**EEP-FRIED **KOFTA** BALLS ARE THE INDIAN VEGETARIAN EQUIVALENT TO MEATBALLS, SERVED WITH SUCCULENT TOMATO OR CURRY SAUCE. THESE **KOFTAS**, MADE WITH POTATOES, PORTOBELLO MUSHROOMS, AND BELL PEPPERS, AND BOUND TOGETHER WITH TRADITIONAL SEASONINGS AND A LITTLE CHICKPEA FLOUR, ARE PAN-FRIED INTO CRISP CAKES. FOR A SPECIAL-OCCASION ENTRÉE, ACCOMPANY THESE GOLDEN BROWN BEAUTIES WITH A SEASONAL VEGETABLE, TOMATO CREAM, AND RICE.

Place the shredded potatoes in a colander and rinse well; set aside to drain. Combine the chickpea flour, baking powder, salt, pepper flakes, garam masala, ginger, almonds, bell pepper, mushroom, and cilantro in a large bowl and toss to mix. Place the potatoes between kitchen towels, press out the excess water, and add them to the dry ingredients. Using your hands, mix until the mixture begins to stick together. Scoop out packed, ½-cup portions of *kofta* mixture and press it between your hands to make 12 flattened balls; set them aside on trays.

Heat ¼ inch of ghee or oil in each of two large, nonstick skillets until hot, but not smoking, then reduce the heat to medium-high. Moisten your palms and flatten each ball slightly to make a pattie, then carefully slip it into the oil. Fry 3 or 4 *kofta* in a pan, without crowding, until they are richly browned, 3 or 4 minutes per side, turning once. Serve at once or transfer to baking trays and keep warm in a 250°F oven for up to 2 hours. To serve, place 2 or 3 *kofta* on each plate and spoon the Tomato Cream over the top.

*2 pounds red potatoes, shredded*

*1½ cups chickpea flour*

*1 teaspoon baking powder*

*½ tablespoon salt*

*½ tablespoon crushed red pepper flakes*

*1 tablespoon garam masala*

*1 tablespoon minced fresh ginger*

*½ cup chopped almonds*

*1 cup diced red bell pepper*

*1 large Portobello mushroom
 (about 8 ounces)*

*½ cup chopped cilantro*

*ghee or peanut oil for frying*

*1 recipe Tomato Cream (page 126),
 heated*

# GRILLED SUMMER VEGETABLES WITH CASHEW CHUTNEY

SERVES 6

**T**HE VAST MAJORITY OF INDIANS COOK OVER WOOD AND COAL EVERY DAY, SO EVEN STOVE-TOP VEG-ETABLE DISHES ARE LICKED BY THE SCRUMPTIOUS FLAVOR OF FIRE AND SMOKE. BEFORE VEGETA-BLES ARE GRILLED, THEY ARE BASTED WITH AN OIL. THIS GINGERY ONE PICKS UP THE FLAVOR OF THE GINGER AND CHILI IN THE MOIST CASHEW CHUTNEY AND IS A FINE COUNTERPOINT TO THE CHARRED, SWEET CARAMELIZED VEGETABLES.

*Cashew Chutney*
⅔ cup dried chana *dal* or yellow
    split peas
½ tablespoon fennel seeds
1 cup cashew nuts
water as needed
½- to 1-inch piece fresh ginger
½ to 3 hot green chilies, seeded
⅓ cup chopped cilantro
salt to taste

⅓ cup ghee or peanut oil
1½ tablespoons grated fresh ginger
½ teaspoon turmeric
2 medium eggplants
12 small new potatoes, steamed
    8 minutes
8 ounces tender okra, trimmed
3 red peppers, quartered and seeded
6 small pattypan squash, halved
salt and cracked pepper to taste
12 Chapatis (page 27) or other flatbread
1 lemon, cut in 6 wedges

For the chutney, place the dal or split peas, fennel seeds, and nuts in a skillet and toast until the dal and nuts brown in a few places. Add 4 cups of water and bring the mixture to a boil for 3 minutes. Set aside for an hour or so, then drain and transfer to a food processor. Pulse until finely chopped. Add the ginger, chilies, cilantro, and 1¼ cups of water. Process until very smooth, for 2 or 3 minutes, adding enough water to make a thin sauce; season with salt. (This chutney will keep for 2 or 3 days refrigerated, and thickens as it sets; thin as desired.)

Place the ghee or oil in a large, deep casserole over medium heat. When it is hot, add the ginger and turmeric; set the pan aside. Cut the eggplants crosswise into slices ½-inch thick. Halve the potatoes. Place the eggplant, potatoes, okra, peppers, and squash in the oil and toss to coat them.

Preheat a charcoal grill or broiler to medium-hot. Arrange the vegetables in grill baskets directly on the grill, or spread them out on baking sheets. Grill or broil, turning as necessary to brown them evenly, until they are cooked through, up to 10 minutes per side depending on the vegetable. As the vegetables cook, transfer them to a warmed platter. Season with salt and pepper. Spread as many chapatis on the grill as will fit, and warm or toast them until char marks fleck both sides; stack in a napkin-lined basket to keep warm.

To serve, distribute the vegetables on 6 plates; add a lemon wedge and a por-tion of chutney to each. Roll the chapatis into cigars and add 2 per plate.

VARIATION: Instead of soaking *chana* or split peas, use 1⅓ cups of drained, cooked chickpeas; briefly toast the fennel and nuts before making the chutney.

# INDIAN VEGETABLE BURGERS

MAKES 24 BURGERS

CALLED VEGETABLE CHOPS IN BENGAL, AND VEG CUTLETS ELSEWHERE, INDIAN VEGGIE BURGERS ARE SERVED EVERYWHERE—IN HOMES, BACK-ALLEY SNACK HOUSES, AND FIVE-STAR HOTEL RESTAURANTS. THESE ARE INSPIRED BY BURGERS SERVED AT THE MAYFAIR RESORT IN JAGANNATHA AT PURI—BEETS (USED FOR A RED BURGER HUE), POTATOES AND OATS (FOR BINDING), COOKED GRAINS AND VEGGIES (FOR TEXTURE), AND SPICES, CHILIES, AND HERBS (FOR FLAVOR, ZEST, AND HEAT). I'VE NEVER HAD ANY TWO BATCHES OF THIS RECIPE TURN OUT EXACTLY THE SAME, SO BE READY TO ADD MORE OATS IF THE MIXTURE IS TOO MOIST, OR MORE CHILIES IF YOU WANT MORE HEAT. DON'T BE PUT OFF BY THE LENGTHY LIST OF INGREDIENTS; THESE BURGERS ARE DELICIOUS, THE YIELD IS GENEROUS, AND THEY FREEZE WELL.

1 tablespoon cold-pressed corn oil

1 tablespoon brown mustard seeds

1 tablespoon cumin seeds

1½ tablespoons grated fresh ginger

1 tablespoon red pepper flakes, or to taste

½ teaspoon yellow asafetida

3 cups finely chopped carrots
   (5 or 6 large)

2 cups finely chopped zucchini
   (2 medium)

3 cups finely chopped yams (3 medium)

3 cups minced beets (3 medium)

2 cups finely chopped turnips
   (2 medium)

2 cups finely sliced green beans

¼ cup flour

4 cups instant rolled oats or 5-grain
   cereal

3 cups cooked white or brown rice

Heat the oil in a large, nonstick skillet over high heat. Drop in the mustard and cumin seeds, and when they begin to pop, add the ginger and red pepper flakes. Fry until the cumin is toasty brown, but not black. Drop in the asafetida and, within 5 seconds, all of the vegetables. Fry for 10 minutes, stirring frequently. Sprinkle in the flour and cook, while stirring, for another 4 or 5 minutes; set aside to cool. To the cooled vegetables in a large bowl, add the oats, rice, potatoes, curry powder, and cilantro. Using your hands, mix well and season with salt and pepper. Using an oiled measuring cup, scoop up ½-cup portions and flatten each into a 3½-inch, smooth-edged pattie. Place the patties on waxed paper–lined baking trays, cover, and refrigerate for at least 4 hours, or better, overnight.

To cook the burgers, place 2 or 3 large, nonstick frying pans over medium-high to high heat. Warm 2 tablespoons of oil in each pan for each batch. Place 3 or 4 burgers in each pan and fry until crisp, richly browned, and charred in places, 4 to 5 minutes per side. Use a gentle hand with the spatula as you turn them over as they break easily at this point. Transfer to cookie racks to cool slightly and firm up while you fry the remaining burgers. (To freeze them, stack cooled burgers between sheets of waxed paper and freeze in dated, well-sealed containers.)

For an entrée, spoon hot Gingered Tomato Sauce on warmed dinner plates and place 2 warm burgers on each; surround with 1 to 4 vegetable dishes (see pages 130–147). For an Indian-style snack, serve with a lime wedge or a spoon of Cashew Chutney (page 116). To serve as burgers, melt a slice of good cheese on top and serve with the works between sliced focaccia, rustic bread, or rolls.

NOTES: You may use more or less oil while frying, but too little will make the crust dry and brittle; nonstick pans keep the burgers from sticking in the pan. I find these burgers are at their best fried in flavored Ghee (page 33) or any type of Consorzio-brand flavored olive oil. Spray the cooked burgers with Tryson's Mesquite Spray just before serving if you like the flavor imparted by an open flame.

4 cups mashed new potatoes

1½ tablespoons curry powder

⅔ cup chopped cilantro or mixed herbs

salt and freshly ground pepper

ghee or extra-virgin olive oil for
   pan-frying

Gingered Tomato Sauce (page 39)

# DHOKRA CAKES WITH WILTED GREENS

**D**HOKRA IS DESCRIBED AS SAVORY CAKE OR SAVORY BREAD, BUT NEITHER DESCRIPTION DOES IT JUSTICE. INDIGENOUS TO GUJARAT, IT IS STEAMED, NOT BAKED, WITH AN AIRY CRUMB BUT MORE SUBSTANTIAL BODY THAN CAKES MADE OF FLOUR. THIS IS BECAUSE **DHOKRA** BATTER IS MADE FROM SOAKED AND GROUND DALS, IN THIS CASE, YELLOW SPLIT PEAS. THIS IS ONE OF MY FAVORITE WAYS TO SERVE **DHOKRA** AS AN ENTRÉE—GRILLED AND SERVED WITH CREAMY BENGALI SWEET AND SOUR **CHANA** DAL (PAGE 83) AND WILTED GREENS.

In separate bowls, rinse the rice and split peas. Cover each with water to a depth of 2 inches, and soak overnight. Rinse and drain the rice and split peas, still keeping them separate. Grind the rice in a food processor until it is powdered. Add the yogurt and process until smooth. Add the drained split peas and process until smooth, 2 or 3 minutes. Scrape the mixture into a bowl and stir in the lime juice, ginger, chilies, salt, asafetida, 3 tablespoons of the chopped cilantro, and just under ½ cup water. The batter should resemble softly whipped cream.

In the bottom of a one- or two-tiered steaming unit, bring plenty of water to a boil. Oil two 8-inch cake pans or twelve 2- to 3-inch, Pyrex custard cups. Strew or arrange the bell pepper over the bottom of the oiled pans or custard cups. Fold the baking soda into the batter to leaven it, and immediately spoon it into the containers. Steam as many *dhokra* containers as will fit in your steamer until the centers firm up, about 12 minutes. After a few minutes, invert the cakes onto a cookie rack. (*Dhokra* may be made 1 or 2 days before use; cover and refrigerate.)

Close to serving time, preheat a grill. Cut each 8-inch *dhokra* cake into 6 wedges, yielding 12 pieces. Dry-toast the mustard seeds until they pop; set aside. Brush melted ghee or butter on all surfaces of the *dhokra* wedges and grill them on both sides until browned and hot. To serve, ladle the hot *chana* dal into large, shallow soup plates, strew hot greens over it, and place 2 wedges or rounds in the center. Sprinkle with mustard seeds.

*3 tablespoons basmati rice*

*1 cup yellow split peas*

*¼ cup yogurt*

*1½ tablespoons lime juice*

*1 tablespoon grated fresh ginger*

*1 or 2 jalapeño chilies, minced*

*1 teaspoon salt*

*¼ teaspoon yellow asafetida (optional)*

*⅓ cup chopped cilantro*

*about ½ cup water*

*⅓ cup each minced green and red*
   *bell pepper*

*ghee or olive oil for the molds and*
   *pan-frying*

*½ teaspoon baking soda*

*ghee or unsalted butter for grilling*

*6 cups Bengali Sweet and Sour Chana*
   *Dal (page 83)*

*Wilted Greens (page 133)*

*½ tablespoon brown mustard seeds*

# SEMOLINA PILAF WITH SEASONAL VEGETABLES

SERVES 6

INSTEAD OF RICE, THIS VEGETABLE-STUDDED PILAF IS MADE WITH SEMOLINA. CALLED **UPPMA**, ITS TEXTURE VARIES FROM FIRM AND POLENTALIKE IN THE SOUTH TO LIGHT AND FLUFFY IN THE NORTH. THIS EXAMPLE OF THE LATTER STYLE IS A SUMMER **UPPMA**, PAIRING THE SMOOTHNESS OF SEMOLINA WITH NUGGETS OF CORN, BELL PEPPERS, AND GREEN BEANS. VARY YOUR CHOICE OF SEASONAL VEGETABLES, USING ONLY ONE OR A FEW VARIETIES, CUT EVENLY SO THEY COOK EVENLY. IF YOU GIVE **UPPMA** A TRY JUST ONCE, YOU'LL PROBABLY BE HOOKED FOREVER. IT'S A GOOD CENTERPIECE DISH FROM BREAKFAST THROUGH LATE SUPPER.

1½ cups semolina or regular farina

3½ cups buttermilk, water, or a
    mixture

½ teaspoon turmeric

1½ teaspoons salt

¼ cup ghee, or 2 tablespoons each corn
    oil and butter

1 tablespoon brown mustard seeds

½ tablespoon cumin seeds

¼ to ½ teaspoon crushed red pepper
    flakes

5 ears corn (3 cups kernels)

2 large diced red bell peppers (2 cups)

8 ounces finely diced green beans
    (2 cups)

¼ cup chopped cilantro or parsley

Pan-toast the semolina or farina over moderate heat until it darkens a few shades, about 8 minutes. Transfer to a pitcher, add the buttermilk or water, turmeric and salt; blend well. Warm half of the ghee or all of the oil in a large, nonstick skillet over high heat. Add the mustard seeds, and when they begin to pop, drop in the cumin seeds and pepper flakes. Cover with a spatter screen. When the seasonings darken, stir in the corn, bell peppers, and beans. Stirring frequently, cook until the vegetables are almost tender, 4 to 5 minutes. Pour in the semolina mixture, stir well, and reduce the heat to medium. Cover and cook, stirring often, until the grains soften and the liquid is absorbed, about 5 minutes. Add more salt if desired. Set aside for another 5 minutes before stirring in the cilantro and the remaining ghee or butter.

# LUCKNOW RED BEAN CHILI

✠

T HE CUISINE OF UTTAR PRADESH IS ROBUST AND EARTHY, AS ILLUSTRATED IN THIS HOME-STYLE CHILI FROM LUCKNOW. CALLED **RAJMA**, IT IS TRADITIONALLY MADE WITH RED KIDNEY BEANS, ALTHOUGH ALMOST ANY KIND OF COOKED BEAN IS PERFECTLY ACCEPTABLE. THOUGH IT IS USUALLY MADE WITHOUT VEGETABLES, A SAUTÉ OF SWISS CHARD OR OTHER VEGETABLE MAKES A NUTRITIOUS ADDITION. SOME RECIPE TASTERS COMMENTED THAT IT HAD A SOUTHWESTERN CHARACTER, BUT IT'S INDIAN, PURE AND SIMPLE. FOR A SATISFYING WINTER MEAL, ACCOMPANY WITH ORANGE CARAMELIZED YAMS (PAGE 145) AND RICE OR CHAPATIS.

2 tablespoons *ghee or corn oil*

½ teaspoon *ajwain seeds*

2 tablespoons *Gujarati Garam Masala*
   *(page 19)*

1 teaspoon *ground chipotle chilies or*
   *pure chili powder*

¼ to ½ teaspoon *yellow asafetida*
   *(optional)*

1½ tablespoons *grated fresh ginger*

one 28-ounce (4 cups) can *crushed*
   *tomatoes*

1½ to 2 cups *bean cooking liquid*
   *or water*

6 to 8 cups *cooked red beans, drained*

salt *to taste*

½ cup *chopped cilantro*

*yogurt or Soured Cream (page 38)*
   *(optional)*

Warm the ghee or oil over very low heat in a heavy-bottomed large pot. Add the *ajwain*, garam masala, chilies, asafetida, and ginger. Stir to prevent the seasonings from scorching and sticking to the bottom of the pot, adding sprinkles of water as necessary, and cook until the mixture is aromatic, 4 to 6 minutes. Pour in 1 cup of the crushed tomatoes, increase the heat to medium, and cook, stirring occasionally, until thickened and the oil oozes out of the tomatoes. This will take about 10 minutes. Add another cup of tomatoes and repeat the process. Add the remaining 2 cups tomatoes, along with the bean cooking broth or water and the cooked beans. Reduce the heat and simmer gently for about 10 minutes. Salt to taste and stir in most of the herbs. Serve garnished with the remaining cilantro, and with or without yogurt or soured cream.

# CHICKPEA AND VEGETABLE STEW

SERVES 6 TO 8

**C**ALLED **KUTTU**, THIS IS A FINE EXAMPLE OF THE SUN-KISSED CUISINE OF KERALA. IN ONE KITCHEN OR ANOTHER, IT HAS BEEN MADE IN DISPOSABLE, BLACK TERRA-COTTA COOKING POTS AND ON THE SAME KIND OF WOODSTOVE FOR CENTURIES. WHEN I LEARNED THIS VERSION, IT WAS WITH OLD-WORLD VEGETABLES—DRUMSTICKS, COLOCASSIA, CHAYOTELIKE SQUASH, GREEN MANGO, PLANTAIN, BABY EGGPLANTS, AND ASPARAGUS BEAN—AND FRESH GREEN CHICKPEAS. I FIND THE DISH WELL SUITED TO IMPROVISATION, REFLECTING TYPICAL SOUTH INDIAN EXUBERANCE IN THE KITCHEN. THIS FALL OR WINTER VERSION OF THE STEW FEATURES SEASONAL PRODUCE. IT IS NOT TOO SPICY AND IS DELICIOUS SERVED WITH CHAPATIS.

Place the chickpeas in a nonstick, 5-quart pot over high heat. Toast the chickpeas until they begin to show traces of color on the edges, 5 or 6 minutes. Cover them with 3 inches of water and soak overnight. Rinse and drain in a colander.

Toast the mustard seeds in the heavy pot until they pop. Add the soaked chickpeas, 8 cups water, ginger, chili or cayenne, tomatoes, curry leaves or bay leaf, and ½ tablespoon of ghee. Bring to a boil. Reduce the heat and boil gently, covered, until the chickpeas are two-thirds cooked, 30 minutes to 1 hour.

While the chickpeas are cooking, trim the eggplants and cut them into 1½-inch cubes. Toss them with the turmeric and salt and set aside for 20 minutes. Scrub and cut the potatoes into 1-inch cubes. Quarter, seed, peel, and cut the pumpkin into 1½-inch cubes.

Rinse and drain the eggplant and add it to the chickpeas, along with the potatoes, pumpkin, and half of the cilantro. Cover and boil gently about 30 minutes; add the shelled beans. Cook until the ingredients are tender, the pumpkin and eggplant melting and breaking down to thicken the stew. Season with salt and pepper.

Heat 2 tablespoons of ghee in a small pan. Fry the fennel and asafetida until the seeds darken a few shades; transfer to the stew. Stir in the remaining cilantro.

1½ cups dried chickpeas

2 teaspoons brown mustard seeds

about 8 cups water

1-inch piece fresh ginger, minced

1 ancho chili, or cayenne powder to taste

1½ cups (a 15-ounce can) diced tomatoes

2 sprigs of curry leaves, or 1 bay leaf

2½ tablespoons ghee or butter

2 medium eggplants (about 2 pounds)

1 teaspoon turmeric

2 teaspoons salt

6 red potatoes (about 1½ pounds)

1 small Sugar pumpkin (about 2 pounds)

½ cup chopped cilantro

1 cup fresh, shelled beans (1 pound unshelled)

salt and freshly ground pepper

½ tablespoon fennel seeds

¼ to ½ teaspoon yellow asafetida

CHAPTER SIX

VEGETABLES

# VEGETABLES

**I**NDIAN VEGETABLE DISHES CAN BE SUMMED UP WITH ONE WORD: VIBRANT. THE ARTFUL APPLICATION OF SPICES MAKES EACH DISH TASTE VIBRANT. The colorful reds, oranges, greens, golds and yellows of bountiful produce make the dishes look vibrant. And the way that food is served all at once, the juxtaposition of small portions of each dish carefully placed to provide contrast, makes the plate look vibrant.

Of course, cooking procedures significantly affect the taste. Most Indian-style vegetables are cooked with dry heat, being pan-fried in seasoned oil, grilled, or roasted. Just try Grilled Okra with Pomegranate (page 131), Roasted Carrots with Garam Masala (page 143), or Green Beans Sautéed in Mustard-Flavored Oil (page 137), to see what I mean. Dry-heat cooking amplifies the flavor of vegetables; when the natural sugars in vegetables caramelize, flavor is concentrated. Few can resist simple Roasted Winter Vegetables (page 146)—tender on the inside and crusty golden on the outside.

By comparison, boiled, blanched, or steamed vegetables often can taste bland, their flavor drained away in the water. When water is used to cook Indian vegetables, it is added after the dish has had its start in seasoned oil, and only enough is added for the finished desired texture—be it dry or moist, a gravy, sauce, or broth.

If you want to create healthy vegetable dishes to your own liking, refer to the descriptions of the three methods for cooking Indian-Style Vegetables (page 30). Using available seasonal produce and this basic information, you will find a whole new horizon of good food opening.

# GRILLED OKRA WITH POMEGRANATE

ON MY LAST TRIP TO INDIA, DETERMINED TO COOK WHILE ON THE ROAD, I LUGGED A PORTABLE PYRAMID STOVE/GRILL AND KITCHEN-IN-A-TRUNK AROUND WITH ME FOR FIVE MONTHS. ON THE SLOPES OF KARNATAKA'S KUTICHAKRA MOUNTAIN, I BROKE IN MY NEW STOVE AND CAME UP WITH THIS DISH ON THE SAME DAY. USING THE ONLY DECENT PRODUCE AVAILABLE IN THE ONE-STREET SHOPPING TOWN OF KOLLUR—OKRA, POMEGRANATES, **NIMBU** LIMES, AND CILANTRO, I DISCOVERED AN UNPLANNED WINNER. GRILLED OVER FRAGRANT WOOD COLLECTED FROM THE FOREST FLOOR UNDER A CANOPY OF STARS IN A BLACK SKY, THIS WAS AN OKRA DISH I VOWED TO SAVOR AGAIN AND AGAIN. ❋ TO MAKE IT, POMEGRANATE JUICE IS REDUCED TO A SYRUPY BASTING SAUCE AND BRUSHED ON OKRA THAT IS GRILLED OR OVEN-ROASTED. PREPARED IN THIS WAY, THE OKRA IS TENDER ON THE INSIDE, WITH A FLAVORFUL GLAZED CRUST ON THE OUTSIDE. TO MY DELIGHT, I RECENTLY NOTED A VERY SIMILAR DISH IN PAULA WOLFERT'S BOOK **THE COOKING OF THE EASTERN MEDITERRANEAN**, THAT VERSION FROM THE MOUNTAINS OF LEBANON. FEW DISHES ARE REALLY NEW, MOST ARE JUST NEW FINDINGS FROM A DISTANT PLACE OR TIME.

Wash the okra and pat it dry with an absorbent towel. Trim the okra tops off and skewer them lengthwise or crosswise. Set aside in a shallow dish.

To make fresh pomegranate juice, roll the fruit around to release the juices inside. Halve and squeeze on a citrus reamer. Strain the juice through a fine sieve. Combine the juice (fresh or bottled), maple syrup, and lemon juice in a nonreactive saucepan and bring to a boil. Lower the heat and reduce the mixture to a syrupy consistency, stirring steadily toward the end to prevent scorching, to yield about 3 tablespoons. Stir in the oil and brush the pomegranate glaze on the okra. Spray both the okra and grill surface with olive oil.

Prepare the grill to medium-hot. Grill until the okra is tender and browned, 10 to 15 minutes depending on size, turning to color evenly. Alternately, preheat the oven to 475°F, spread the okra out in a single layer on baking trays, and roast until browned. Spray with additional oil and season with salt. Sprinkle with cilantro and serve hot.

*2 pounds small, bright green okra*

*3 pomegranates, or ¾ cup bottled pomegranate juice*

*2 tablespoons maple syrup*

*1 tablespoon fresh lemon juice*

*2 tablespoons cold-pressed peanut oil*

*olive-oil spray*

*salt or Orange-Chili Salt (page 22)*

*3 tablespoons chopped cilantro*

# ROASTED POTATOES WITH CURRY LEAVES

SERVES 4 AS A MAIN DISH; 8 AS A SIDE DISH

LIKE ALL ROASTED POTATOES, THESE ARE CRUSTY ON THE OUTSIDE AND TENDER INSIDE. WHAT MAKES THEM SO OUTSTANDING AND CHARACTERISTICALLY INDIAN ARE THE SPICES IN THE ROASTING PAN—FRESH CURRY LEAVES AND GINGER ROOT, FENNEL SEEDS, AND TURMERIC. I FIRST ENJOYED THESE TUBERS TWENTY YEARS AGO WITH THICK FRESH YOGURT AND FLAME-TOASTED CHAPATIS. THIS IS A GOOD SMALL MEAL, ANY TIME, ANY PLACE.

8 large Yukon Gold, Yellow Finn, or
   baking potatoes (3 pounds)
extra-virgin olive-oil spray
20 fresh curry leaves, or 2 bay leaves
½ tablespoon fennel seeds, crushed
½ teaspoon turmeric
1½ tablespoons grated fresh ginger
¾ cup water or vegetable stock
1 teaspoon coarse kosher salt
paprika or cayenne powder
juice of half a lime

Preheat the oven to 400°F. Choose a baking dish large enough to hold the potatoes in a single layer and spray it with oil. Peel the potatoes and place them in cold water. Cut a thin slice off the long side of a potato (if it is oval), so it lies flat on a cutting board. Place a wooden spoon on each long side of the potato. Leaving ½ inch at both ends, carefully make slices at ⅛-inch intervals, from one end to the other, cutting down until the knife rests on the wooden spoons, so the potato, although partially sliced, stays intact. Pat the potatoes dry and arrange them, cut-side up, in the baking dish. Spritz the potatoes with olive oil.

Mix the curry leaves, fennel seeds, turmeric, ginger, and water or stock and pour the mixture over the potatoes. If using bay leaves, slip them in between the potatoes. Sprinkle the potatoes with coarse salt and spritz them again with olive oil.

Basting them every 10 or 15 minutes with the liquid, roast the potatoes for 40 to 50 minutes, or until they are fork tender and most of the stock is cooked off. Finish off with a sprinkle of paprika or cayenne, the lime juice, and an additional spritz of olive oil.

# WILTED GREENS

SERVES 4

**S**AAK, GREEN VEGETABLE DISHES LOVED THROUGHOUT INDIA, ARE MADE DIFFERENTLY FROM REGION TO REGION. NUTRITIONISTS ARE QUICK TO POINT OUT THE FOOD VALUE OF GREENS, BUT FOR COOKS, IT'S THE CRISP PUNGENCY OF THEIR FLAVOR THAT'S THE HOOK. IN THE NORTH, **SAAK** DISHES ARE BUTTERY, CREAMY, AND RICH, AND FRIED **PANIR** CHEESE OR FRIED POTATOES MAY BE ADDED. THE EASTERN APPROACH IS SIMPLER — THE GREENS ARE FLASH-COOKED IN A FLAVORED OIL. THIS WORKS WITH MANY, EVERYDAY VARIETIES OF GREENS SUCH AS SPINACH, KALE, GREEN OR RED CHARD, MUSTARD, AND COLLARDS AND WITH UNUSUAL ASIAN VARIETIES, SUCH AS BOK CHOY, **TAK SOI**, PAK CHOI, AND MIZUNA. FOR VARIETY, COLOR, AND TEXTURE, ADD FRESH CORN KERNELS, THINLY SLICED SNOW PEAS, GREEN OR YELLOW STRING BEANS, OR BABY PEAS.

Remove the coarse stems from the greens and reserve them for another use. Stack the leaves, roll them up, and slice them crosswise into thin slivers. Heat 1 teaspoon of ghee or oil in a large, nonstick pan or wok. Drop in the mustard seeds and, when they just begin to pop, add the pepper flakes. When the flakes darken slightly, pile on the wet greens. Sauté until they are wilted, slightly soft, and bright green, anywhere from 3 to 8 minutes depending on the variety. Season with salt and pepper and drizzle with the remaining teaspoon ghee or oil.

*2½ pounds greens, washed*

*2 teaspoons ghee or extra-virgin olive oil*

*½ tablespoon brown mustard seeds*

*¼ to ½ teaspoon red pepper flakes*

*salt and freshly ground pepper*

# CHILI-MASHED POTATOES WITH FRIED GINGER

❈

SERVES 6

THIS ZESTY RECIPE WILL ONLY ADD TO YOUR LOVE OF POTATOES. THE BUTTERMILK GIVES THEM A RICH CREAMINESS, THE CHILIES A LITTLE WARMTH, AND THE NUGGETS OF CRISP, FRIED GINGER AND GINGER-FLAVORED GHEE A SCRUMPTIOUS TASTE.

2½ pounds baking potatoes

½ to 2 jalapeño chilies, seeded and chopped

1½ cups buttermilk or yogurt

salt and freshly ground pepper

3 or 4 tablespoons ghee or unsalted butter

3 tablespoons minced fresh ginger

2 tablespoons chopped cilantro for garnishing

Peel the potatoes and cut them in 1-inch pieces. Cook the potatoes in a large pot of boiling water until tender, about 25 minutes. Drain, and using a potato masher, mash them coarsely. Add the chilies and buttermilk or yogurt and continue to mash or beat until the mixture is smooth. Season with salt and pepper.

Warm the ghee or butter and ginger in a small pan over medium heat. Cook, stirring occasionally, for 3 minutes. Swirl into the potatoes and serve piping hot, garnished with cilantro.

# CURRIED EGGPLANT AND SPINACH

✦

SERVES 6 TO 8

LEAFY GREEN DISHES, CALLED **SAAK**, ARE POPULAR THROUGHOUT INDIA. EGGPLANT AND SPINACH ARE AN ESPECIALLY POPULAR COMBINATION, IN SOME REGIONS COOKED UNTIL THE VEGETABLES MELT INTO EACH OTHER, AND IN OTHERS, LEFT TEXTURED, AS IN THIS VERSION FROM MAHARASHTRA. OVEN-ROASTING THE EGGPLANT GIVES IT THE RICH FLAVOR OF THE FRIED, BUT REQUIRES FAR LESS OIL. THIS IS A FINE SIDE-DISH VEGETABLE FOR RICE OR DAL, BUT EQUALLY DELICIOUS AS AN ENTRÉE WITH PASTA AND A DUSTING OF GRATED DRY MONTEREY JACK CHEESE.

Preheat the oven to 400°F. Peel and cut the eggplants into ½-inch cubes. Quarter, seed, devein, and cut the peppers into 1-inch pieces. Combine the eggplant, peppers, chickpea flour, turmeric, 1 tablespoon of the garam masala, salt, and half of the ghee or oil in a bowl. Pour in the water and toss to mix. Spread the vegetables in a single layer on two baking sheets and spray them with olive oil. Roast the vegetables until they are browned and tender; 20 to 25 minutes. Set aside.

Heat the remaining ghee or oil in a large, nonstick skillet over medium-high heat. Add the mustard seeds and fry until the seeds pop. Add the ginger, chilies, cardamom, sweetener, and tomatoes and stir-fry until the tomatoes are somewhat pulpy; 4 or 5 minutes. Add the spinach, cover, and cook until the spinach is bright green and softened. Stir in the eggplant, season with salt and spritz with olive oil.

VARIATION: To serve with pasta, add ½ cup slivered, black, oil-cured or Niçoise olives with the spinach.

*3 medium eggplants (1½ pounds)*

*3 yellow bell peppers (1½ pounds)*

*¼ cup chickpea flour*

*1 teaspoon turmeric*

*2 tablespoons Garam Masala*
  *(page 19)*

*1½ teaspoons salt*

*2 or 3 tablespoons ghee or extra-virgin*
  *olive oil*

*½ cup water*

*olive-oil spray*

*1½ tablespoons brown mustard seeds*

*2 tablespoons grated fresh ginger*

*1 to 3 hot green chilies, minced*

*½ teaspoon cardamom seeds, crushed*

*1 tablespoon Sucanat (raw cane sugar)*
  *or granulated sugar*

*2 pounds plum tomatoes, seeded and*
  *coarsely chopped*

*1½ pounds spinach, trimmed and*
  *chopped*

# GUJARATI VEGETABLES WITH LIME AND CILANTRO

SERVES 4 AS A MAIN DISH; 6 TO 8 AS A SIDE DISH

THIS BEAUTIFUL GUJARATI STIR-FRY IS PACKED WITH FLAVOR AND COLOR AND IS IDEAL FOR SUMMER ENTERTAINING. THE VEGETABLES CAN BE PREPARED WELL BEFORE THEY ARE NEEDED, AND SAUTÉED IN A SPICE-FLAVORED OIL JUST BEFORE SERVING. THE DISH IS FINISHED OFF WITH THE GUJARATI FLAVORING TRIO OF LIME JUICE, SUGAR AND CILANTRO. HERE THE PRINCIPLE IS APPLIED TO A FEW VEGETABLES SUPPLIED BY MY ORGANIC GARDENER — STEAMED FINGERLING POTATOES, GREEN BEANS, YELLOW SQUASH, AND RED BELL PEPPERS. ON DAYS WHEN IT'S TOO HOT TO COOK MORE THAN ONE DISH, THIS VEGETABLE DISH MAKES A SATISFYING MEAL.

1 pound potatoes, steamed and peeled

3 yellow summer squash
   (about 1 pound)

½ pound green beans

1 red bell pepper

1 tablespoon ghee or avocado oil

1 teaspoon each cumin seeds, coriander
   seeds, and fennel seeds

¼ to ½ teaspoon red pepper flakes

½ teaspoon turmeric

salt and freshly ground pepper to taste

2 teaspoons fructose or sugar

juice from 1 lime

3 tablespoons chopped cilantro

Keeping them separate, halve the potatoes and squash and slice them ¼-inch thick. Trim the green beans and cut them in half. Seed and devein the pepper and cut in long thin strips.

Heat the ghee or oil in a large, nonstick frying pan on medium-high heat. Drop in the cumin, coriander, and fennel and, when they begin to darken, add the pepper flakes and turmeric. Fry for a few seconds, then add the summer squash and green beans. Stirring occasionally, sauté until the vegetables are half cooked, about 2 minutes. Add the potatoes and bell pepper and continue to cook until the squash is tender-crisp; 3 or 4 minutes. Season with salt and pepper and add the sugar. Stir-fry for another minute or two, then remove from the heat. Sprinkle with lime juice and garnish with cilantro.

# GREEN BEANS SAUTÉED IN MUSTARD-FLAVORED OIL

✳

SERVES 6

**M**ADE IN THE SOUTH INDIAN **PORIYAL** STYLE, THESE GREEN BEANS ARE DRY-TEXTURED, WITH MOIST BITS OF CORIANDER AND THE COCONUT AND DAL MASALA CLINGING TO THEM, GLISTENING IN A GINGER AND MUSTARD-FLAVORED OIL. INSTEAD OF GREEN BEANS, TRY YELLOW STRING BEANS, CLUSTER BEANS, YARD-LONG BEANS, SHELLED LIMA BEANS, BROAD BEANS, OR FAVA BEANS, WHATEVER IS FRESH AND AVAILABLE. SERVE BEAN **PORIYAL** PIPING HOT AS A VEGETABLE DISH OR AT ROOM TEMPERATURE AS A SALAD.

To make the masala, place the oil, *chana* dal or split peas, chilies, and coriander seeds in a large, nonstick skillet over medium-high heat. Stirring frequently, toast until the legumes darken a few shades; 3 to 4 minutes. Transfer the ingredients to a blender and pulse until the mixture is coarsely powdered. Add the coconut and water and continue to process until smooth, 2 to 3 minutes. Dry coconut will absorb more water than fresh or frozen; add water as necessary to make a thin purée.

Place the coconut masala in a nonstick skillet over medium-high heat. Cook, stirring occasionally, until the masala is dry. Add the beans and warm thoroughly. Season with salt and pepper.

In a small pot, heat the oil over moderate heat. Add the ginger and mustard seeds and cook until the seeds pop. Serve, garnished with a drizzle of the infused oil, cilantro, and lime juice.

*Coconut-Dal Masala*

1 teaspoon cold-pressed nut or
    vegetable oil
⅓ cup split chana *dal* or yellow
    split peas
¼ to ½ teaspoon dried red pepper flakes
1½ tablespoons coriander seeds
½ cup fresh, frozen, or dried
    grated coconut
2 cups water

2 pounds green beans, finely cut ⅓-inch
    thick and steamed until tender
salt and freshly ground pepper
1 or 2 tablespoons cold-pressed vegetable
    or nut oil
½ tablespoon grated fresh ginger
½ tablespoon brown mustard seeds
3 tablespoons chopped cilantro or
    flat-leaf parsley
1 tablespoon fresh lime juice

# PUNJABI PAN-FRIED FRESH BEANS

SERVES 6

I'VE SAMPLED BEANS MADE THIS WAY IN MANY KITCHENS, AND MY FAVORITES INCLUDE RAW GREEN CHICKPEAS AND DICED YARD-LONG BEANS. IF YOU HAVE ACCESS TO A GOOD FARMERS' MARKET, PICK UP ANY INTERESTING VARIETY THAT LOOKS ESPECIALLY FRESH. WHEN TESTING THE RECIPE, I USED DRAGON TONGUE WAX BEANS, WHICH HAVE FLAT GOLDEN PODS WITH VIOLET STRIPES, THIN **FILET** (FRENCH) BEANS, PURPLE-BROWN SCARLET RUNNERS, AND ROMANO BEANS. ABSENT THE UNUSUAL, EVEN THE UBIQUITOUS SUPERMARKET GREEN BEANS TASTE VERY GOOD THIS WAY IF THEY ARE TENDER.

*1 cup water*

*½ cup chickpea flour*

*2 teaspoons Garam Masala (page 19)*

*1 teaspoon salt or to taste*

*1½ pounds tender green beans*

*2 tablespoons ghee or peanut oil*

*½ teaspoon brown mustard seeds*

*¼ teaspoon* ajwain *seeds*

*¼ to ½ teaspoon red pepper flakes*

*3 tablespoons chopped cilantro*

Whisk together ½ cup of the water, the chickpea flour, garam masala, and salt. Trim and cut the beans into ¼- to ½-inch lengths.

Heat 1 tablespoon of the ghee or oil in a large, nonstick skillet over medium-high heat. Drop in the mustard and *ajwain* seeds and red pepper flakes. When the mustard seeds pop or the seeds darken, drop in the beans. Fry briefly, then add the remaining water. Reduce the heat, cover, and cook until the beans are almost tender.

Stir the beans, then pour the chickpea flour batter around the edge of the pan. Do not stir, but cook until it firms up to make a crêpelike ring, about 2 minutes. Now add the remaining tablespoon ghee and the cilantro, gently stir all the contents of the pan, and fry until the batter forms little browned nuggets, 5 or 6 minutes. Add salt if necessary.

# SAUTÉED SUGAR SNAPS AND RADISHES IN FENNEL-FLAVORED OIL

SERVES 4

I LIKE TO MAKE THIS DISH, OR ONE VERY MUCH LIKE IT, AT COOKING DEMONSTRATIONS IN STORES. CURIOUS PASSERSBY ARE LURED IN FIRST BY ITS DELICIOUS SMELL. THEN THEY BECOME ENTRANCED BY THE FLAVOR, OFTEN BUYING SPICES ON THE SPOT TO MAKE SIMILAR DISHES AT HOME. ❉ INSTEAD OF USING THESE SPRING VEGETABLES, USE OTHER VEGETABLES IN SEASON—ASPARAGUS, EGGPLANT, YELLOW SQUASH, ZUCCHINI, BELL PEPPERS, WILD MUSHROOMS, RAW CORN KERNELS, PEAS, SNOW PEAS, PARSNIPS, OR FENNEL BULB—WITH ADJUSTMENTS IN COOKING TIMES. SERVE AS A SIDE-DISH VEGETABLE, SCATTERED OVER SALAD GREENS, FOLDED INTO PLAIN COOKED BEANS, OR AS PART OF A COMPOSED VEGETABLE PLATTER.

Warm the ghee or olive oil in a large sauté pan over moderate heat. Drop in the fennel seeds and ginger and fry until the seeds darken a few shades. Add the peas, radishes, and a sprinkle of water. Cook briefly until the color intensifies; 1 to 3 minutes. Season with salt and pepper and garnish with cilantro.

2 teaspoons ghee or extra-virgin olive oil

1 teaspoon fennel seeds

1 teaspoon grated fresh ginger

1 pound sugar snap peas, strings removed

8 white radishes, trimmed and thinly sliced

8 red radishes, trimmed and thinly sliced

salt and freshly ground pepper

2 teaspoons slivered cilantro leaves for garnishing

# ROASTED CARROTS WITH GARAM MASALA

SERVES 4 TO 6

**M**Y ITALIAN GRANDMOTHER'S EXCELLENT ROASTED CARROTS WERE FRAGRANT WITH ROSEMARY AND OLIVE OIL, AND CARROTS ARE SIMILARLY OUTSTANDING WHEN ROASTED WITH INDIAN MASALAS AND GHEE. I CAME UP WITH THIS VERSION ON MY LAST WINTER PILGRIMAGE TO VRINDAVANA'S GOVARDHANA HILL, WHERE THE GIANT ORANGE CARROTS IN THE BAZAAR ARE ESPECIALLY SWEET AND FINE TEXTURED. AS THE CARROTS ROAST, SWEET GUJARATI GARAM MASALA AND FRESH ORANGE AND LIME JUICES REDUCE TO A CITRUS GLAZE. A FINE DISH FOR DINNER OR HOLIDAYS.

Preheat the oven to 400°F. Peel the carrots and slice on the diagonal about 1-inch thick. Combine the citrus juices, garam masala, and ghee or butter in a large casserole or 11-by-14-inch baking dish. Add the carrots and roast until tender and lightly browned, stirring a few times, for 25 to 30 minutes. Serve garnished with currants and lime zest.

*2 pounds large carrots*

*1 cup fresh orange juice*

*juice and finely grated zest of 1 lime*

*1½ tablespoons Gujarati Garam Masala (page 19)*

*1 tablespoon ghee or butter*

*1 tablespoon dried currants*

# CURRIED CAULIFLOWER

SERVES 4 TO 6

CAULIFLOWER CURRY, STANDARD FARE IN INDIAN RESTAURANTS, IS OFTEN OVERCOOKED AND GREASY, A POOR REFLECTION OF THE FINE VERSIONS COOKED IN NORTH INDIAN HOMES. TO AID DIGESTION AND BRING OUT ITS FLAVOR, CAULIFLOWER SHOULD BE COOKED QUICKLY, SAUTÉED IN SPICE-FLAVORED GHEE, AND THEN ALLOWED TO CONTINUE COOKING IN ITS OWN JUICES, WITHOUT ADDITIONAL WATER, UNTIL EACH FLORET IS SUCCULENT AND CARAMELIZED. EATEN WITH FLAME-TOASTED CHAPATIS, IT'S A SIMPLE FEAST. CERTAINLY GIVE THE DISH A TRY IN THE FALL, WHEN LOCAL, SNOWY WHITE CAULIFLOWERS START SHOWING UP IN VEGETABLE MARKETS.

*1 large cauliflower (2 pounds)*

*1 tablespoon coriander seeds*

*1 teaspoon cumin seeds*

*½ teaspoon fennel seeds*

*2 or 3 tablespoons ghee or oil*

*1-inch piece fresh ginger, peeled and finely julienned*

*¼ teaspoon cayenne powder or paprika*

*½ teaspoon turmeric*

*½ tablespoon sugar*

*salt and freshly ground pepper*

*3 tablespoons chopped cilantro*

Trim and divide the cauliflower into even-sized, very small florets. In a mortar, pound the cumin, coriander, and fennel until crushed. Heat all but 1 teaspoon of the ghee or oil in a nonstick wok or 5-quart pan over medium-high heat. Stir in the ginger and fry it for about 20 seconds, then add the crushed spices, cayenne, turmeric, sugar, and a sprinkle of water. Within seconds, add the cauliflower and stir-fry for 2 or 3 minutes. Reduce the heat to low, cover, and cook to the desired tenderness, shaking the pan occasionally; 15 to 20 minutes. Season with salt and pepper, drizzle with the remaining ghee or oil, and garnish with cilantro.

VARIATION: Warm ½ cup buttermilk, yogurt, or Soured Cream (page 38) and fold it in just before serving.

# ORANGE CARAMELIZED YAMS

SERVES 6

MY FRIEND ERIK SCHWARTZ BROUGHT HIS PARENTS, BOTH GARDENERS AND COOKS, TO LUNCH THE DAY I FINISHED TESTING THIS RECIPE. WHEN I ASKED FOR THEIR OPINION, I GOT AN ENTHUSIASTIC SIX THUMBS UP AROUND THE TABLE. IN SPITE OF THE FRESH GINGER AND HOMEMADE CURRY POWDER, THESE YAMS DON'T TASTE INDIAN; THEY JUST TASTE GOOD, AND CALL FOR VERY LITTLE OIL. JEWEL YAMS OR RED GARNET SWEET POTATOES ARE GOOD CHOICES, THE YAMS A LITTLE SWEETER TO MY TASTE.

Preheat the oven to 400°F. Peel the yams or sweet potatoes, and cut them into roughly 1¼-inch cubes. Combine the yams with the ghee, curry powder, ginger, citrus juices and zest, and maple syrup in a glass, ceramic, or metal baking dish, and toss to mix. Bake, basting and gently tossing a few times, until the yams are tender, about 1 hour. Season with salt and pepper. If the juice has not reduced to a thick sauce, pour it into a small pan and cook it for a few minutes until it is thick. Fold the juice glaze into the tubers. Fold in the cilantro.

2½ pounds yams or sweet potatoes

2 teaspoons ghee or extra-virgin olive oil

½ teaspoon curry powder, preferably homemade (page 18)

1 tablespoon grated fresh ginger

juice from 1 lime

zest and juice from 2 oranges

¼ cup maple syrup

salt and freshly ground pepper

2 tablespoons chopped cilantro

# ROASTED WINTER VEGETABLES

OUT-OF-SEASON, SHRINK-WRAPPED IMPORTED VEGETABLES ARE NOW AVAILABLE IN SOME VEG-ETABLE BAZAARS IN DELHI AND BOMBAY, BUT VILLAGERS STILL RELY ON JUST-PICKED PRODUCE FROM LOCAL FARMERS. IN MOST RURAL INDIAN MARKETS IN WINTER, POTATOES, CARROTS, AND PUMP-KINS ARE WIDELY AVAILABLE, AS THEY ARE HERE. THESE THREE VEGETABLES ARE TERRIFIC ROASTED, THEIR SUGARS CARAMELIZING, THEIR BROWNED EXTERIORS FULL OF FLAVOR. WHEN I HAVE A CHOICE OF VARIETY, I USE ORGANIC SUGAR PUMPKINS, YUKON GOLD POTATOES, AND SCARLET NANTES CARROTS, SOMETIMES ADDING SLICED PORTOBELLO MUSHROOMS. EQUALLY GOOD ARE SUPERMARKET YAMS, PARSNIPS, TURNIPS, SWEET POTATOES, BABY BEETS, AND JERUSALEM ARTICHOKES. ROASTED VEGETABLES ARE SO EASY, SO NICE, AND SO GOOD.

⅓ to ½ cup ghee, peanut oil or extra-
virgin olive oil

1 tablespoon brown mustard seeds

1 teaspoon fennel seeds

½ teaspoon red pepper flakes

1 small Sugar pumpkin (2 pounds)

4 waxy potatoes (1½ pounds)

6 medium carrots (1½ pounds)

4 medium Portobello mushrooms
(optional)

salt and freshly ground pepper

½ cup chopped cilantro

juice from 1 lemon or lime

Preheat the oven to 475°F. In a large pot, heat the ghee or oil and mustard seeds over medium heat. When the seeds begin to pop, drop in the fennel seeds and pepper flakes; remove from the heat in 5 or 10 seconds. Cut the pumpkin in eighths. Peel the segments, and cut them into slices ½-inch thick. Steam the pumpkin for about 5 minutes, then add it to the oil. Halve the potatoes, slice ½-inch thick, and add them to the oil. Slice the carrots on the diagonal ¾-inch thick, and add them to the oil. Season with salt and pepper and toss to mix. Spread the vegetables in a single layer on 2 nonstick baking trays. Roast until the vegetables are tender and browned, turning twice; 25 to 35 minutes. If you roast mushrooms, slice the caps ½-inch thick and toss in the spiced oil left over from the other vegetables. When the vegetables are about two-thirds cooked, sprinkle the mushrooms onto the trays and continue roasting until the mushrooms are softened and browned; 10 minutes or so. Sprinkle all the vegetables with the lemon or lime juice before serving and garnish with cilantro.

AJWAIN: Also known as *ajowan* and, in English, bishop's weed. The same size as celery, *ajwain* is a close relative of cumin and caraway and has a flavor like thyme. It is used predominantly in northern India.

ASAFETIDA: A dried gum resin obtained from several species of *Ferula* (the same genus as fennel). It tastes like garlic or onion. Use only the mild, yellow asafetida compound.

BASMATI RICE: Literally "queen of fragrance," this rice, grown for millennia in the foothills of the Himalayas, is considered by many to be the finest in the world. The long, pointed grains have a fragrant, nutty bouquet when aged.

BITTER MELON: Known as *kerela* in India, bitter melons are typically between four and eight inches long, thick in the middle, tapering to pointed ends, and green in color with wrinkled skin. Large bitter melons are less bitter than small ones; avoid yellow or spongy bitter melons.

CHANA DAL: A split and husked relative of the chickpea or garbanzo bean, this *dal* and the flour derived from it are widely used, especially in Bengal. Also known as Bengal *gram*.

CHAPATI: An unleavened flatbread made from whole wheat flour and water. It is baked on a griddle and then placed over an open flame to inflate it.

CHONK: Spices and seasonings fried alone, or together, until their aroma and flavor intensifies. They can be added at the beginning, middle, or end of cooking. A spice-seed *chonk* might be flash-fried over lively heat; a wet-paste *chonk* might be fried over very low heat for 5 to 10 minutes.

CHUTNEY: Piquant, usually very hot Indian relishes that serve as enhancers or accents to other dishes. Can be either fresh or cooked. Fresh chutneys are made with herbs, nuts and seeds; cooked ones are made with fruits or tomatoes.

CURRY LEAVES: The leaves of *Murraya koenigii*, known in India as *kadhi patta* or *mitha neem patta*, are delightfully fragrant and are used to flavor many classic Indian dishes.

CURRY POWDER: A popular South Indian spice blend in which fenugreek seeds and fresh curry leaves predominate. It is now widely used in all cuisines.

DAL: Any type of dried bean, pea or lentil; see *chana* dal, mung dal, *toor* dal, and *urad* dal. Also, the name of any cooked legume dish.

DALPURI: A flaky, deep-fried pastry stuffed with chili-laced ground *urad* dal; popular in North India.

DHOKRA: A steamed, not baked, savory bread made with a batter of soaked and ground legumes; indigenous to Gujarat.

DOSA: A South Indian unleavened, thin pancake or crêpe. May be made from batters of ground rice and legumes or flours.

FRUCTOSE: Natural sugar derived from fruit.

GARAM MASALA: Literally "a warm spice mixture," usually combining three or more traditionally so-called warm spices, such as ginger, cardamom, black pepper, cinnamon, cloves, coriander, cumin, fennel, and chilies, which are known to fuel the fire of digestion.

GHEE: Butter that has been clarified so that all of the milk solids are removed, leaving only the pure butterfat, which can be heated to high temperatures for frying and sautéing.

KITCHEREE: An earthy, richly-seasoned stew made with dals and rice. Eaten every day by many people in India, this popular stew provides a delicious, protein-rich, satisfying meal with minimal effort.

KOFTA: The Indian vegetarian equivalent to meatballs.

MASALA: Literally "a spice blend," traditional masalas run the gamut from prized family recipes to the universally known blends, such as *sambar* masala, garam masala, or *chaat* masala.

MUNG DAL: Whole and split beans of *Vigna radiata*, also known as green *gram*. The whole beans are green and the split are yellow, with a delicate flavor.

MUSTARD SEEDS: Thin, round seeds from various mustard plants. Small, brown seeds, available at Indian grocers, are preferred by Indian cooks for their superior flavor. Yellow seeds are pleasantly warm and widely available.

PAKORA: Fritters made with virtually any vegetable coated in a chickpea-flour batter and deep-fried until golden and tender-crisp.

PANIR: An easily digested, unripened fresh cheese with a consistency similar to that of fresh mozzarella and a taste similar to that of farmer cheese.

PAPPADAM: A sun-dried, paper-thin, unseasoned wafer made from mung dal or *urad* dal. Available at Indian markets and some supermarkets.

SAMBAR DAL: A traditional South Indian soup made with *toor* dal and a distinctive spice blend. Can be mildly suggestive of warmth or searingly hot, usually the latter when served in India.

SAMBAR MASALA: A distinctive spice blend designed to flavor South Indian *sambar* dal.

SAMOSA: A vegetable- or fruit-filled pastry, traditionally deep-fried.

SUCANAT: Raw cane sugar that is similar to the Indian unrefined sugar known as *gur*. Moist and dark brown, it lends both flavor and sweetness to a dish.

TOOR DAL: A split lentil seed of *Cajunus cajan* (pigeon pea in English), with a delightful, slightly sweet taste.

TURMERIC: The dried, ground rhizome of *Curcuma domestica*. The bright yellow orange color gives a warm hue to dals, sauces, legumes, and vegetable dishes. An essential spice in Indian cooking, but to be applied sparingly; can be bitter if overused.

URAD DAL: A bean, *Vigna mungo*, also known as black *gram*, this protein-rich, close relative of the mung bean is widely used in both its whole and split forms throughout India.

# INDEX

✻

# TABLE OF EQUIVALENTS

✷

THE EXACT EQUIVALENTS IN THE FOLLOWING TABLES HAVE

BEEN ROUNDED FOR CONVENIENCE.

## US/UK

oz = ounce
lb = pound
in = inch
ft = foot
tbl = tablespoon
fl oz = fluid ounce
qt = quart

## METRIC

g = gram
kg = kilogram
mm = millimeter
cm = centimeter
ml = milliliter
l = liter

## WEIGHTS

| US/UK | Metric |
|---|---|
| 1 oz | 30 g |
| 2 oz | 60 g |
| 3 oz | 90 g |
| 4 oz (¼ lb) | 125 g |
| 5 oz (⅓ lb) | 155 g |
| 6 oz | 185 g |
| 7 oz | 220 g |
| 8 oz (½ lb) | 250 g |
| 10 oz | 315 g |
| 12 oz (¾ lb) | 375 g |
| 14 oz | 440 g |
| 16 oz (1 lb) | 500 g |
| 1½ lb | 750 g |
| 2 lb | 1 kg |
| 3 lb | 1.5 kg |

## OVEN TEMPERATURES

| Fahrenheit | Celsius | Gas |
|---|---|---|
| 250 | 120 | ½ |
| 275 | 140 | 1 |
| 300 | 150 | 2 |
| 325 | 160 | 3 |
| 350 | 180 | 4 |
| 375 | 190 | 5 |
| 400 | 200 | 6 |
| 425 | 220 | 7 |
| 450 | 230 | 8 |
| 475 | 240 | 9 |
| 500 | 260 | 10 |

## LIQUIDS

| US | Metric | UK |
|---|---|---|
| 2 tbl | 30 ml | 1 fl oz |
| ¼ cup | 60 ml | 2 fl oz |
| ⅓ cup | 80 ml | 3 fl oz |
| ½ cup | 125 ml | 4 fl oz |
| ⅔ cup | 160 ml | 5 fl oz |
| ¾ cup | 180 ml | 6 fl oz |
| 1 cup | 250 ml | 8 fl oz |
| 1½ cups | 75 ml | 12 fl oz |
| 2 cups | 500 ml | 16 fl oz |
| 4 cups/1 qt | 1 l | 32 fl oz |

## LENGTH MEASURES

| | |
|---|---|
| ⅛ in | 3 mm |
| ¼ in | 6 mm |
| ½ in | 12 mm |
| 1 in | 2.5 cm |
| 2 in | 5 cm |
| 3 in | 7.5 cm |
| 4 in | 10 cm |
| 5 in | 13 cm |
| 6 in | 15 cm |
| 7 in | 18 cm |
| 8 in | 20 cm |
| 9 in | 23 cm |
| 10 in | 25 cm |
| 11 in | 28 cm |
| 12 in/1 ft | 30 cm |

### All-purpose (plain) flour/ dried bread crumbs/chopped nuts

| | | |
|---|---|---|
| ¼ cup | I oz | 30 g |
| ⅓ cup | I½ oz | 45 g |
| ½ cup | 2 oz | 60 g |
| ¾ cup | 3 oz | 90 g |
| I cup | 4 oz | 125 g |
| I½ cups | 6 oz | 185 g |
| 2 cups | 8 oz | 250 g |

### Whole-Wheat (Wholemeal) Flour

| | | |
|---|---|---|
| 3 tbl | I oz | 30 g |
| ½ cup | 2 oz | 60 g |
| ⅔ cup | 3 oz | 90 g |
| I cup | 4 oz | 125 g |
| I¼ cups | 5 oz | 155 g |
| I⅔ cups | 7 oz | 210 g |
| I¾ cups | 8 oz | 250 g |

### Brown Sugar

| | | |
|---|---|---|
| ¼ cup | I½ oz | 45 g |
| ½ cup | 3 oz | 90 g |
| ¾ cup | 4 oz | 125 g |
| I cup | 5½ oz | 170 g |
| I½ cups | 8 oz | 250 g |
| 2 cups | 10 oz | 315 g |

### White Sugar

| | | |
|---|---|---|
| ¼ cup | 2 oz | 60 g |
| ⅓ cup | 3 oz | 90 g |
| ½ cup | 4 oz | 125 g |
| ¾ cup | 6 oz | 185 g |
| I cup | 8 oz | 250 g |
| I½ cups | 12 oz | 375 g |
| 2 cups | I lb | 500 g |

### Raisins/Currants/Semolina

| | | |
|---|---|---|
| ¼ cup | I oz | 30 g |
| ⅓ cup | 2 oz | 60 g |
| ½ cup | 3 oz | 90 g |
| ¾ cup | 4 oz | 125 g |
| I cup | 5 oz | 155 g |

### Long-Grain Rice/Cornmeal

| | | |
|---|---|---|
| ⅓ cup | 2 oz | 60 g |
| ½ cup | 2½ oz | 75 g |
| ¾ cup | 4 oz | 125 g |
| I cup | 5 oz | 155 g |
| I½ cups | 8 oz | 250 g |

### Dried Beans

| | | |
|---|---|---|
| ¼ cup | I½ oz | 45 g |
| ⅓ cup | 2 oz | 60 g |
| ½ cup | 3 oz | 90 g |
| ¾ cup | 5 oz | 155 g |
| I cup | 6 oz | 185 g |
| I¼ cups | 8 oz | 250 g |
| I½ cups | 12 oz | 375 g |

### Rolled Oats

| | | |
|---|---|---|
| ⅓ cup | I oz | 30 g |
| ⅔ cup | 2 oz | 60 g |
| I cup | 3 oz | 90 g |
| I½ cups | 4 oz | 125 g |
| 2 cups | 5 oz | 155 g |

### Jam/Honey

| | | |
|---|---|---|
| 2 tbl | 2 oz | 60 g |
| ¼ cup | 3 oz | 90 g |
| ½ cup | 5 oz | 155 g |
| ¾ cup | 8 oz | 250 g |
| I cup | II oz | 345 g |

### Grated Parmesan/Romano Cheese

| | | |
|---|---|---|
| ¼ cup | I oz | 30 g |
| ½ cup | 2 oz | 60 g |
| ¾ cup | 3 oz | 90 g |
| I cup | 4 oz | 125 g |
| I⅓ cups | 5 oz | 155 g |
| 2 cups | 7 oz | 220 g |